100 YE

MW01126136

NOTES

including
- *Life of the Author*
- *Introduction to the Novel*
- *The Buendía Genealogy*
- *List of Characters*
- *Critical Commentaries*
- *Character Analyses*
- *Themes and Motifs*
    Solitude
    Fantasy
    Cyclical Time and Fate
    Illegitimacy
    Machismo vs Heroism
    Prophecy
- *Essay Topics*
- *Selected Bibliography*

by
Carl Senna, Instructor
  of Expository Writing
Harvard College

INCORPORATED
LINCOLN, NEBRASKA 68501

Editor

Gary Carey, M.A.
University of Colorado

Consulting Editor

James L. Roberts, Ph.D.
Department of English
University of Nebraska

ISBN 0-8220-0964-1
© Copyright 1984
by
Cliffs Notes, Inc.
All Rights Reserved
Printed in U.S.A.

1997 Printing

Cliffs Notes, Inc.   Lincoln, Nebraska

CONTENTS

100 YEARS OF SOLITUDE NOTES

LIFE OF THE AUTHOR

Gabriel García Márquez (nicknames: Gabo, Gabito) was born March 6, 1928. Like the strange banana town of Macondo in *One Hundred Years of Solitude*, his home was a tiny Colombian village called Aracataca, near the Caribbean coast. He seems not to have known his father and did not meet his mother until he was almost eight years old. He was raised by his grandparents, who, in his words, were "the most decisive literary influence for me. After the death of my grandfather [when García Márquez was eight years old], nothing really happened to me any more." When a reporter once asked him where he got his rich, yet pungent style, he replied: "It's the style of my grandmother."

The author's grandfather, who became the model for "the Colonel" in the novel and the short stories, had participated in the civil war known as "The War of a Thousand Days." It was a traumatic event in Colombia's historical consciousness. Following the signing of the peace treaty, a revolution suddenly erupted and the country lost its Panama territory, the canal zone. A United States-backed republic arose in its place. Before this time, the village of Aracataca had vegetated along in almost total isolation from the world. Like the fictional Macondo, the village of Aracataca had been founded by Colombian civil war refugees, and when the United Fruit Company established a banana headquarters there, Aracataca became the scene of many labor protests and massacres. Eventually the banana company was forced to leave. All this becomes material for the action in the author's fiction.

In 1940, García Márquez left Aracataca for Bogotá, where he attended a Jesuit school. After graduation he began to study law at the University of Bogotá, but found, as he says, that law "had nothing to do with justice." When political violence closed the university, he transferred his studies to the city of Cartagena; he was, at best, a desultory student. He began working as a journalist there and in the port town of Barranquilla. From 1950 to 1952, he wrote a column called "La Jirafa" ("The Giraffe") for *El Heraldo* in Barranquilla. His writings at the time were heavily spiced with the irony and mordant humor so characteristic of his later fiction. His first published stories, however, appeared in 1947 while he was a student at Bogotá. Quitting law school, he moved to Barranquilla, where he became involved with a small group of writers and newsmen who knew his work. He had now turned altogether to journalism, taking a job as a newspaper columnist. In 1954, he returned to Bogotá as a film critic and reporter for the Colombian newspaper *El Espectador*.

"As a reporter," he once said, "I was the lowest on the paper and wanted to be. Other writers always wanted to get to the editorial page but I wanted to cover fires and crimes." He appeared then, as critic William Kennedy put it, to have "as much Ben Hecht as Hemingway in him." (See "The Yellow Trolly Car in Barcelona and Other Visions – a Profile of García Márquez," *Atlantic,* Jan. 1973.) One might add that he also had a touch of Barnum and Bailey showmanship in him as well. Once an *El Espectador* correspondent falsely reported a rebellion in Quibdo, a remote jungle village, and García Márquez and a photographer were dispatched there. They arrived after very difficult travel through the bush only to discover a sleepy village and the correspondent trying to find relief from the heat in a hammock. The story had been faked to protest the correspondent's assignment. With the help of sirens and drums, García Márquez gathered a crowd and took action photos of a staged rebellion. When he sent back his "story," an army of reporters arrived to cover the "rebellion."

Perhaps the most important point in his career as a newspaper-man came in 1966 when a sailor named Luis Alejandro Velasco came to *El Espectador* to tell of his incredible survival at sea. An editor on the paper suggested that the sailor talk to García Márquez. Alejandro was a survivor of a Colombian naval destroyer crew which was struck by storm en route home from New Orleans. The survival was already well-publicized, but only newspapers friendly to Colombian dictator Gustavo Rojas Pinilla had been permitted interviews with Alejandro. García Márquez' interview turned out to be a fourteen-chapter exposé, narrated in the first-person and signed by the twenty-year-old seaman. Among other revelations, the sailor reported that the destroyer had not encountered a storm at all but, instead, had been carrying black market goods on deck. High winds had knocked the cargo loose and the eight victims who survived, including Alejandro, had been knocked overboard during the storm. These facts, which turned out to be substantially true, made the article an instant success but deeply embarrassed the government. Later, the account was published in book form under García Márquez' name in 1970, the first time he was credited with authoring the piece. The title of the book was: *The Tale of A Shipwrecked Sailor, who was adrift ten days on a life raft without food or water, who was proclaimed a hero of the nation, kissed by beauty queens and made rich by publicity, and then loathed by the government and forgotten forever.*

In 1954, García Márquez was assigned to the Vatican as a correspondent for *El Espectador.* He had just completed *Leaf Storm (La Hojarasca),* his first serious writing, and he planned to become a director and film his own version of *Leaf Storm.* After some months of study he moved to Paris and learned that the Rojas Pinella dictatorship had closed *El Espectador* and that he was jobless. He stayed in Paris and began a short story about violence. His language became more resonant and more rhythmic, with dialogue appearing more frequently than before. His long short story expanded quickly into a short novel (*Leaf Storm*), then two more novels appeared, the last which he completed first; it became *No One Writes to the Colonel (El Coronel No Tiene Quien Le Escriba).* He rewrote *No One Writes to the Colonel* eleven times; his first novel about violence was called *La Mala Hora (The Evil Hour).* In Paris, García Márquez said he lived on "daily miracles." He was a foreigner, not permitted to work, unable to speak French very well, and had run out of cash. He was living on credit in a Latin Quarter hotel and owed some 123,000-odd francs. He once said that he re-boiled chicken bones to make broth for his daily meals. The hotel, sensing his desperate straits, never tried to collect. The management trusted him, so he says, because they saw him working in his room the whole time. This kind of hand-to-mouth existence continued until one night when he sneaked into a maid's room. He was caught, but his new landlord let him live in an attic when his money ran out so that he was able to continue writing. Looking back on these three years of poverty, he concluded: "If I had not lived those three years, probably I would not be a writer. Here I learned that nobody dies of hunger and that one is capable of sleeping under bridges." In 1957, he sold newspaper editors in Bogotá and Caracas on the idea of a series of ten articles about the socialist Eastern European countries. Subsequently, he returned to Colombia to marry his fiancée, Mercedes, the model for the Mercedes of the "beautiful neck and sleepy eyes" in *One Hundred Years of Solitude*. (This fictional Mercedes is also engaged to a fictional Gabriel.)

García Márquez then moved to Venezuela when a newsman on a socialist country tour, Plinio Apuleyo Mendoza, became editor of *Momento*, a Caracas magazine, and hired young García Márquez. It was there in Caracas, as he reported on the last days of the Perez Jimenez dictatorship, that he finished *Big Mama's Funeral (Los Funerales de la Mama Grande)*, a collection of short stories published in Mexico in 1962. Only one story is set in Macondo, however; the rest are set in an unnamed town ("El Pueblo"). He left *Momento* and went to work for *Venezuela Grafica*, a magazine sometimes called *Venezuela Pornografica* in Caracas because it resembles both *Playboy* and *Penthouse*. García Márquez, needless to say, was not put off by the non-literary quality of his work. "I'm interested in personal life," he said, "I read all the gossip in all the magazines. And I believe it all."

After the Cuban revolution, he opened the Bogotá office for *Prensa Latina*, Cuba's revolutionary news agency. He had been a socialist since his militant student days at the University. Then, in 1960, he represented *Prensa Latina* at the United Nations' Fifteenth General Assembly – the same year former Russian Premier Nikita Khruschev used his shoe as a gavel there. He visited Havana and in 1961 went to New York to become *Prensa Latina's* assistant bureau chief. He resigned during an internal dispute concerning party ideology, leaving with his boss after only a few months in New York City. He says that his visa was withdrawn by U. S. immigration authorities while he was preparing to leave with his wife and son, Rodrigo, for Mexico City. This experience was to embitter him for some time afterwards. "New York," he said later, "was responsible for withdrawing my visa. As a city, New York is the greatest phenomenon of the twentieth century, and therefore it's a serious restriction of one's life not to be able to come here every year, even for a week. But I doubt if I have strong enough nerves to live in New York. I find it so overwhelming. The United States is an extraordinary country; a nation that creates such a city as New York, or the rest of the country – which has nothing to do with the system or the government – could do anything."

When García Márquez received his visa back, he left immediately for Mexico City, going by Greyhound bus through the Deep South "in homage to Faulkner, with my books under my arms." He noted signs on the way advising that dogs and Mexicans were prohibited; he thus found himself barred from hotels because of his dark Latin complexion, the bigoted clerks mistaking him for a Mexican. Upon being served a "filet mignon with a peach and syrup on top of it" in New Orleans, he fled to Mexico City without further delay. In Mexico City ("with only a hundred dollars in my pockets"), he began slowly, and with great difficulty, a new career as a screen writer. He wrote film scripts, some in collaboration with Mexican novelist Carlos Fuentes; several of these scripts became movies. One of his stories, "There are No Thieves in This Town," was filmed by an experimental group for presentation at the 1965 Locarno Film Festival. At other times he worked as an editor and once did publicity for the J. Walter Thompson office in Mexico City. During this period – almost six years – he wrote only one short story. "It was a very bad time for me," he has confessed, "a suffocating time. Nothing I did in films was mine. It was a collaboration, incorporating everybody's ideas, the director's, the actor's. I was very limited in what I could do and I appreciated then that in the novel the writer has complete control." Meanwhile, his friends had arranged for his two recent books to be published. In 1961, *The Evil Hour (La Mala Hora)*, which had been completed in Mexico but initially published in Spain, had been published, but only after he had won a Colombian literary prize. The original title of the novel had been *Este Pueblo de Mérida (The Town of Dung)*. The title was changed at the suggestion of the author's friends but not without some objection from García Márquez.

García Márquez had now written four books of literary merit: the novels *Leaf Storm* (1955) and *The Evil Hour* (1961); a novella entitled *No One Writes to the Colonel* (1961); and a short story collection, *Big Mama's Funeral* (1962). In January of 1965, while driving from Mexico City to Acapulco, he began plans for *One Hundred Years of Solitude*. Though promising enough, all his previous works can be seen as but preliminary exercises to this masterpiece. He later told an Argentinean writer that he could have dictated an entire chapter on the spot if he had had a tape recorder. He went home and told his wife: "Don't bother me, especially don't bother me about money." And he began writing the work, which he says he had been brooding over since he was sixteen. His desk was called the "Cave of the Mafia"; there, he worked for eight to ten hours a day for eighteen months. When he had finished the novel, his wife informed him that they owed twelve thousand dollars. She had sustained them by borrowing from friends, paying for groceries on monthly installments and not paying any rent to the landlord for six months. García Márquez says that he again began writing, "straight off without a break, and afterwards made a great many corrections on the manuscript, made copies, and corrected it again." Now, however, he corrects line by line as he works. He dates his interest in writing to an impulse to draw comics as a child.

García Márquez sent the first three chapters of *One Hundred Years of Solitude* to Carlos Fuentes, who along with the Argentinean writer Julio Cortázar was an early fan and supporter. Fuentes was so impressed that he wrote to a Mexican magazine: "I have just finished reading the first seventy-five pages of *Cien Años de Soledad*. They are absolutely magisterial." *One Hundred Years of Solitude* was published initially in Buenos Aires, Argentina, in 1967 by Editorial Sudamericana. It was translated into English by Gregory Rabassa, a winner of the National Book Award for his translation of Julio Cortázar's *Hopscotch*. In 1970, *One Hundred Years of Solitude* was published in English by Harper & Row. It drew universal critical acclaim and won the Prix du Meilleur Livre Etranger in France in 1969; that same year it also won Italy's coveted literary award, the Premio Chianciano. In 1970, the novel was chosen as one of the twelve best books of the year by many American critics; in 1972, García Márquez won the Rómulo Gallegos Prize in Venezuela and the Books Abroad/Neustadt International Prize for Literature. Finally, he was awarded the 1982 Nobel Prize in Literature. In his Nobel lecture in Stockholm, he declared: "This, my friends, is the very scale of our solitude . . . in spite of this, to oppression, plundering and abandonment, we respond with life. Neither floods nor plagues, nor famines nor cataclysms, nor even the eternal wars of century upon century have been able to subdue the persistent advantage of life over death. . . . On a day like today, my master William Faulkner said 'I decline to accept the end of man.' I would feel unworthy of standing in this place that was his if I were not fully aware that the colossal tragedy he refused to recognize thirty-two years ago is now, for the first time since the beginning of humanity, nothing more than a simple scientific possibility.

Faced with this awesome reality that must have seemed a mere utopia through all of human time, we, the inventors of tales, who will believe anything, feel entitled to believe that it is not yet too late to engage in the creation of the opposite utopia."

INTRODUCTION TO THE NOVEL

Of all the works by García Márquez, this novel is the most fascinating and the most complex. From the very beginning we recognize the same elements – albeit, more elaborate ones – as those of the characters and situations in his shorter fiction. In the words of the Peruvian author Mario Vargas Llosa: "*One Hundred Years of Solitude* extends and magnifies the world erected by his previous books." Indeed, the novel is a brilliant amalgamation of elements from all of García Márquez' previous stories, including elements from the fiction of other American novelists, biblical parables, and personal experiences known only to the author.

The basic structure of the novel traces the chronicle of the Buendía family over a century. It is the history of a family with inescapable repetitions, confusions, and progressive decline. Beginning sometime in the early nineteenth century, the novel's time span covers the family's rise and fall from the foundation of Macondo by the youthful patriarch, José Arcadio Buendía, until the death of the last member of the line. Throughout the narrative, the fates of the Buendías and Macondo are parallel reflections. In fact, we witness the history of a people who, like the wandering tribes of Israel, are best understood in terms of their genesis from a single family.

One Hundred Years of Solitude exaggerates events and personal characteristics to such a degree that it is very difficult to define its predominant aim. Sometimes it seems to be satire; at other times it appears to be an evocation of the magical. Perhaps we can be safest in observing that the novel demonstrates that the line between fantasy and reality is very arbitrary. It shows, for instance, that our sense of technical and material progress is relative, and that backwardness, for instance, can be caused as much by social isolation as by historical distance in time. Everything depends upon one's cultural reference. A commonplace telescope is a fabulous instrument to either people isolated from modern civilization, or, at some time or another, to all children.

One Hundred Years of Solitude consists of twenty unnumbered chapters or episodes. The first chapter narrates the genesis of the Buendía clan in the fictional town of Macondo. The story begins in the memory of Colonel Aureliano Buendía, son of Macondo's founder, as he recalls the first time that his father took him to "discover ice." The Colonel's memory evokes a pristine world, but this moment is overshadowed by the fact that he is facing a firing squad. At once, the omniscient narrator makes us aware that we are in the memory of a character as well as listening to a historical myth. Having lived in physical isolation, as well as psychological solitude, the people of Macondo learn about "progress" from the wandering gypsies – one of whom, Melquíades, possesses a manuscript in Sanskrit code which contains the history and fate of the Buendía family. This narrative will be the manuscript which is being decoded by the last adult Buendía just before he dies. The novel will constantly shift through time, so that memory and linear, chronicle time are mixed together in order to give the action a mournful, ghostly tone.

The Colonel's childhood memory – as he faces an execution squad – introduces us to the irony of Macondo, an ebullient jungle village which time had once forgotten and which was located at a point that seemed "eternally sad." In the beginning, before "progress" came to Macondo, José Arcadio Buendía and his wife, Úrsula, because they were cousins, lived in fear of begetting a child with a pig's tail. We are told that a boy with such a tail had been born to Úrsula's aunt and José Arcadio Buendía's uncle. This fear is later to be realized in the love affair between the only remaining Buendías, the bookish Aureliano Babilonia and his aunt, Amaranta Úrsula. Incest, then, becomes the original sin which threatens six succeeding generations of Buendías. From the fear of having a baby with a pig's tail, the novel's principal theme of solitude is psychological, as much as geographical; Their hereditary fear gives them an irrational zeal for the fantastic, and it cripples their ability for sincere love and honest communication.

After her marriage to José Arcadio Buendía, Úrsula refuses to consummate their union for fear of conceiving a monster. She wears a chastity belt to prevent her husband from having intercourse with her. One day, however, José Arcadio Buendía defeats a poor loser in a cockfight. Prudencio Aguilar taunts the young Buendía about Úrsula's virginity, an insult that is aimed at José Arcadio's manhood. José Arcadio, in an impetuous rage, throws an ancient spear through

Aguilar's throat and kills him. Úrsula later sees the dead man's ghost trying to plug the hole in his throat with "a plug of esparto grass." Aguilar's ghost haunts the couple until they are forced to flee their ancestral village. Thus, the Buendías set out with some of their friends on a long journey through the jungle. Two exhausting years later, after camping in the wilds one night, José Arcadio Buendía has a dream about a city of houses with mirrored walls. He takes this dream as a divine sign, and he convinces his followers to build Macondo on the very site.

When José Arcadio Buendía, his wife Úrsula, and some twenty other adventurers settle there, the world is said to be so recent that many things do not have names and thus "it was necessary to point." José Arcadio organizes his small settlement into a model community. Yet there is already something strange about it. José Arcadio had planned the streets so as to shade all the homes from the tropical sun, but Macondo remains a burning place where the hinges and door knockers melt with the heat, "a peninsula surrounded by water where water was never known to be." When a heat wave occurs in Macondo, men and beasts go mad and birds attack houses; later, the town is afflicted by a plague of insomnia and, even later, things have to be labeled. Eventually these labels have to be placed in the context of a thing's function. Occurring shortly after Rebeca's mysterious arrival, the insomnia plague not only causes the loss of memory but prevents sleep. The result is that the townspeople stay up nights amusing one another with nonsensical tales like the one about the capon:

> an endless game in which the narrator asked if they wanted him to tell them the story about the capon, and when they answered yes, the narrator would say that he had not asked them to say yes, but whether they wanted him to tell them the story about the capon, and when they answered no, the narrator told them that he had not asked them to say no, but whether they wanted him to tell them the story about the capon, and when they remained silent the narrator told them that he had not asked them to remain silent but whether they wanted him to tell them the story about the capon . . . and so on and on in a vicious circle.

As the names and uses of things are being lost, José Arcadio builds a primitive computer dictionary. But Melquíades, the gypsy, returns to Macondo with a cure for the insomnia plague when José Arcadio has programmed fourteen thousand entries. The destruction of memory, like senility, signals the beginning of the transformation of consciousness; the insomnia plague is a metaphor for Macondo's prehistoric innocence, just as its cure is the mark of its cyclical return to history, to irreversible chronological and psychological time, and to a move out of a fantastic isolation.

This fabulous setting is the stage for the action of the novel as it relates to the Buendías. As in the Bible, the beginnings of things are in the words that bring them to the light of human consciousness. Hence, the narrative starts in the memory of how a child discovers for the first time something which is quite commonplace and yet which we know will be discovered by all children for all time to come. In this case, the child is not only the Colonel but his father as well, the patriarch José Arcadio Buendía, who has a childlike fascination with things which were commonplace to all other people except the Macondians.

THE BUENDÍA GENEALOGY

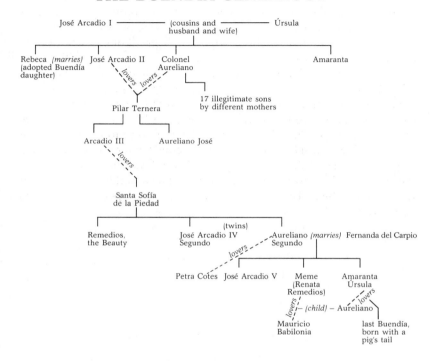

LIST OF CHARACTERS

José Arcadio Buendía

The patriarch of the Buendía clan is the discoverer of Macondo. Over the objection of relatives, he has married his cousin Úrsula Iguarán. The two families had been intermarrying for centuries in a small town. Near the eve of their wedding the couple is warned that consummation of the marriage may result in children with pigs' tails, or child-iguanas. Úrsula becomes frigid while José Arcadio takes up cockfighting. After an insult following a cock bout, he kills Prudencio Aguilar, whose ghost causes the couple to seek refuge in Macondo. José Arcadio becomes the father of the later Colonel Aureliano Buendía.

Colonel Aureliano Buendía

Aureliano Buendía is the first human born in Macondo. "Silent and withdrawn," his fetus weeps in Úrsula's womb. His eyes are open at birth. Clairvoyant, he is possessed of prophetic powers. He impregnates his brother's mistress, Pilar Ternera, who bears his son, Aureliano José. The Colonel casts the longest shadow in the novel. As the most outstanding member of the second generation, it is through his triumphs and failures that we come to understand the theme of solitude.

José Arcadio II

José Arcadio II is the oldest child of José Arcadio and Úrsula Buendía. At the age of fourteen, his prodigious sexual development stirs Úrsula's latent, newlywed fears of years past. Soon enough he becomes the lover of the fortune teller Pilar Ternera, attracted to her, so we are told, "by the smell of smoke" under her armpits and skin. To avoid confusion, their son is called "Arcadio," although baptized as "José Arcadio." Arcadio saves the Colonel from execution by firing squad. His own death, however, is violent yet ambiguous.

Aureliano Segundo, the twin of José Arcadio Segundo

The male character next to the Colonel in significance is the son of Santa Sofía de la Piedad and Arcadio. He is also the twin brother of José Arcadio Segundo and younger brother of Remedios the Beauty. The Colonel, therefore, is his uncle. His story begins midway in the novel, in the retrospective future, a technique that parallels the beginning of the novel: "Years later on his death bed Aureliano Segundo would remember the rainy afternoon in June when he went into the bedroom to meet his first son."

José Arcadio Segundo IV, Aureliano's twin

Both twins reflect, in the words of critic Jack Richardson, "the melancholy transition" of Macondo. But if Aureliano is a genial lover of orgies, a reckless no-good, and a creature of passion, José Arcadio proves to be a fanatic who reacts against injustice out of moral outrage; he is impulsive and enterprising "but marked with a tragic sign." He also has a morbid interest in executions. He and his brother fulfill the Buendía legacy of tragic forerunners, doomed to failure and solitude yet achieving a perpetuation of the line.

Aureliano Babilonia, the last adult Buendía

Aureliano Babilonia is the illegitimate offspring of Renata Remedios (Meme) and Mauricio Babilonia, the auto mechanic. Aureliano takes up the obsessive quest of José Arcadio IV Segundo, his great-great-grandfather, in deciphering the parchment manuscript containing the Buendía family's destiny and history. He and Amaranta Úrsula are the parents of the baby Aureliano, a child who fulfills the prophetic curse of Buendía incest when he is born with "the tail of a pig."

"Arcadio": José Arcadio III

Pilar Ternera and José Arcadio II, the son of the patriarch, have a son who is baptized José Arcadio, but who is called Arcadio in order to avoid confusion. He is almost the same age as Amaranta Buendía, and the two of them grow up together learning to speak the Guajiro Indian language from a servant. He becomes "the cruelest ruler that Macondo had ever known."

Aureliano José

The illegitimate child of Pilar Ternera and Colonel Aureliano Buendía, Aureliano José is the oldest child of the Colonel's family. He falls hopelessly in love with his aunt, Amaranta. His fate is to fall to wreaking vengeance, and his death becomes a testament of family-blood solidarity.

José Arcadio V, son of Aureliano Segundo

The asthmatic, insomniac son of Fernanda del Carpio, José Arcadio V is sent off to Rome to realize Úrsula's wish to have *one* José Arcadio not only a priest – but Pope!

Aureliano, born with the tail of a pig, the last of the Buendías

At the end of the novel, this baby is carried off by giant ants. He is the last of the family line, the offspring of the incestuous relationship between Aureliano Babilonia and his aunt, Amaranta Úrsula. He fulfills the ancient Buendía fear, first expressed in the novel by Úrsula Iguarán, that incest would eventually produce a child with a pig's tail.

The Seventeen Sons of Colonel Buendía

Colonel Aureliano Buendía has seventeen bastard sons by different mothers. One day they all turn up at the Buendía house, all bearing the name "Aureliano" and the last name of their mothers.

Úrsula Iguarán

The pillar of the Buendías is the wife of Macondo's founder, José Arcadio Buendía. Like her husband, she comes from an old South American family and lives in a sleepy coastal village. During the trek to Macondo, she gives birth to José Arcadio II.

Pilar Ternera

Although she is not a Buendía, Pilar Ternera is next to Úrsula in importance. She becomes the mistress, first of José Arcadio II, then of Aureliano. She bears Arcadio III for José Arcadio II and gives birth to Aureliano José for the Colonel. She is summed up best in terms of wasted beauty: "Fat, talkative, with the airs of a matron in disgrace."

Fernanda del Carpio

She is the first and most important female character of the third generation. She appears as the intruding Queen of Madagascar during the carnival celebration over which Remedios the Beauty already reigns. Aureliano Segundo marries her. She is a nervous, rigidly formal woman who tries unsuccessfully to ignore her husband's affair with Petra Cotes.

Petra Cotes

Fernanda's rival (or alter ego) is characterized as being a clear opposite. Petra Cotes is not from Fernanda's antique lineage, nor does she have her rival's false pride. She is "the clean young mulatto woman with yellow almond-shaped eyes that give her face the ferocity of a panther." She is the mistress of both Aureliano Segundo and his brother, José Arcadio Segundo IV, with whom she sleeps first.

Rebeca Buendía

She is the adopted daughter of José Arcadio I and Úrsula Buendía. She comes from a town called Manaure, and the narrative reveals her as the second cousin of the Buendía matriarch. She is José Arcadio II's wife against the wishes of her adopted family.

Amaranta Buendía

The natural daughter of José Arcadio I Buendía and Úrsula is a strange, perverse creature. She is born "light and watery, like a newt, but all her parts were human." She becomes the rival of her step-sister, Rebeca, for the affection of the Italian pianola expert, Pietro Crespi.

Santa Sofía de la Piedad

She is the young virgin who is paid 50 pesos by Pilar Ternera so that Ternera may avoid committing incest with her son, Arcadio III. Santa Sofía and Arcadio III have a daughter at the time Arcadio becomes "dictator" of Macondo. Besides the girl (Remedios), Santa Sofía has the twins, José Arcadio Segundo and Aureliano Segundo, also fathered by Arcadio.

Renata Remedios (Meme)

The eldest daughter of Fernanda del Carpio and Aureliano Segundo is born into the hostile atmosphere of the Buendía quarrel because of her mother's arrogance and pride. Only Fernanda calls her Renata; the others call her Meme, the diminutive of Remedios. She and Mauricio Babilonia, the auto mechanic, are the parents of Aureliano Buendía.

Remedios the Beauty

The daughter of Santa Sofía and Arcadio III has no name for eight months, until just before her father's execution. She becomes known as Remedios the Beauty when she and her brothers, the Segundo twins, begin school.

Remedios Moscote

Aureliano marries the youngest daughter of Don Apolinar Moscote, Macondo's Conservative mayor. At the time of her betrothal, Remedios is so young that she has not even had her first menstrual period and still wets her bed. She has the first set of Buendía twins, who die stillborn and are the cause of her death.

Nigromanta

Nigromanta is the daughter of one of the West Indian Negroes who live segregated, off from Macondo; she becomes the mistress of Aureliano Babilonia and Gabriel Márquez.

Mercedes

The girl "with the stealthy beauty of the Nile, thin neck and sleepy eyes" is the pharmacist's daughter. She gives Aureliano the asthma medicine for José Arcadio V, and she is the fiancée of Gabriel Márquez.

Camila Sagastume

The woman who engages Aureliano Segundo in an eating contest.

Big Mama

Big Mama is a character from García Márquez's story "Big Mama"; she is merely a reference in the novel.

Visitacíon

Visitacíon is the first Buendía house-servant, a Guajiro Indian who (with her brother Cataure) comes to Macondo in flight from an insomnia plague.

Argénida

Rebeca's servant; she leads the authorities to the dead body of her mistress.

Tranquilina Buendía

Tranquilina María Miniata Alacoque Buendía is the grandmother whom the blind, aged Úrsula thinks she sees just before she dies.

Petronila Iguarán

Petronila Iguarán is Úrsula's great grandmother. She appears as a hallucination in the blind matriarch's old age.

Melquíades

Melquíades is the most important presence in the novel outside the major Buendía male and female characters. He is the gypsy friend of José Arcadio Buendía I, and introduces Macondo to a host of fabulous things. The gypsy's Sanskrit manuscript turns out to be the narrative of the Buendías.

The Parchment Manuscript

The manuscript that Melquíades gives to José Arcadio Buendía is cryptic looking; its writing looks "like pieces of clothing put out to dry on a line."

Prudencio Aguilar, The Ghost of the Past

He is the poor loser in a cockfight with José Arcadio Buendía and the indirect cause of Macondo's being founded. José Arcadio kills him with a spear, and the dead man's ghost haunts Úrsula and the patriarch until they flee their ancestral village.

Father Nicanor Reyna

The first priest in Macondo, he gives dispensation to José Arcadio II and Rebeca to be married.

Father Coronel ("The Pup")

When Father Nicanor is consumed by hepatic fever, he is replaced by the young idealist, Father Coronel. "The Pup," as he is called, is a veteran of the first federalist war.

Father Antonio Isabel

Father Coronel is replaced by Father Antonio Isabel. It is Isabel who daubs the indelible ash crosses on the seventeen Aurelianos, an act seemingly which marks them for death.

Father Agusto Ángel

Father Isabel's replacement is a crusader of the "new breed" but is soon worn out by the sleepiness of Macondo.

Don Apolinar Moscote

Don Apolinar Moscote is the first Conservative mayor of Macondo and the father of Remedios.

Colonel Gerineldo Márquez

He is the friend and constant supporter of Colonel Aureliano Buendía and great-great-grandfather of Gabriel Márquez, Aureliano Babilonia's friend.

Gabriel Márquez

Aureliano Babilonia's friend is Babilonia's link with the memory of Colonel Aureliano Buendía. He becomes Nigromanta's lover and the fiancé of Mercedes. The great-great-grandson of Colonel Gerineldo Márquez is an earnest competitor in a quiz contest offering a free trip to Paris.

Pietro Crespi

The Italian pianola expert, "young and blond, the most handsome and well-mannered man who had ever been seen in Macondo," is engaged by Úrsula to teach Rebeca and Amaranta how to dance. He meets a tragic end, but later his brother Bruno Crespi becomes a prosperous merchant in Macondo and introduces a cinema to the town.

Mr. Herbert

Mr. Herbert is the man most responsible for bringing the banana company to Macondo.

Mr. Jack Brown

He is the president of the banana company. His daughter Patricia Brown befriends Meme. Brown is, according to the narrator, responsible for one of Macondo's worst floods.

Gaston

The Belgian husband of Amaranta Úrsula; he enters Macondo led in tow on a silken leash. He leaves Amaranta to Aureliano and decides to set up a palm oil business in the Belgian Congo.

Magnífico Visbal

The other close friend of the Colonel is Magnífico Visbal. Visbal and his grandson are murdered by the police after the Treaty of Neerlandia has been signed, a treaty that supposedly gives the rebels amnesty.

The Wise Old Catalonian

The owner of the bookstore in Macondo where Aureliano obtains the Sanskrit dictionary; the old bookseller is the first to see the futility of Macondo's existence.

Aureliano Triste

Aureliano Triste is the one Aureliano of the Colonel's seventeen illegitimate sons who emerges as a character. He sets up the ice factory dreamed of for so long by José Arcadio Buendía I. He also opens a channel from the world to Macondo and drives in the first locomotive, a huge yellow huffing, puffing monster.

Cataure

The Guajiro Indian servant and brother of Visitación; like his sister, Cataure comes to Macondo in flight from the insomnia plague.

Catarino's Store

Catarino's store is a place of ill-repute in Macondo and seemingly a legitimate place of business, as well.

Liberals vs. Conservatives

The two contending parties that form the civil war are the Liberals and Conservatives. The Buendías are all Liberals – except, possibly, José Arcadio II Segundo. The Liberals are symbolized by the color red and the Conservatives by blue.

The Duke of Marlborough

The historical character who is said to have aided the Colonel during the war.

The French Doctor

He corresponds with letters (perhaps only imaginatively) with Fernanda.

The Keys of Nostradamus

The symbol of Melquíades' extraordinary knowledge.

Francisco the Man

The composer of the songs played by Aureliano Segundo on his accordion.

Rafael Escalona

He carries on the memory of Francisco the Man by playing and singing the latter's songs.

Sir Francis Drake

It is suggested that the Spanish galleon found by José Arcadio Buendía in the jungle may have been sunk by Sir Francis Drake ("the attacker of Riohacha").

Aureliano Amador

The last of the seventeen bastard sons of the Colonel to be killed.

The Hotel Jacob

Macondo's only hotel. It also appears in García Márquez' story "One Day After Saturday."

Aureliano Centeno

One of the seventeen illegitimate sons of the Colonel, he invents sherbet.

Mauricio Babilonia

The auto mechanic who fathers Aureliano with Meme. He is paralyzed for life by a guard's bullet as he tries to rendezvous with Meme in her bathroom.

The Wandering Jew

Father Isabel claims to have seen this legendary wanderer in support of his "proof" of the devil.

Dr. Alirio Noguera

A medical charlatan, "a false homeopath," who instigates a Liberal rebellion and starts the Colonel on the path of revolution.

Teófilo Vargas

A "Liberal" terrorist leader who is executed by the Colonel.

Captain Roque Carnicero

The would-be executioner of Colonel Aureliano Buendía. He joins the Colonel's forces after José Arcadio II stops the execution in a dramatic rescue.

General Victorio Medina

Revolutionary leader of the Liberals. He is shot before the Colonel can join him.

Captain Aquiles Ricardo

The Conservative garrison commander of Macondo. He orders the execution of Aureliano José and is himself shot four hours before the former's death.

Carmelita Montiel

A fortune card teller and twenty-one-year-old virgin. Her future with Aureliano José expires when he is killed.

CRITICAL COMMENTARIES

One Hundred Years of Solitude has twenty unnumbered chapters. For the sake of convenience, I have numbered the sections 1 through 20.

SECTIONS 1 – 4

The novel begins in the retrospective present – that is, as Colonel Aureliano Buendía faces a firing squad, he remembers the first time that his father took him to "see ice." The omniscient narrator will describe most of this novel through the *memories* of its various characters. Thus, we are introduced almost at once to the novel's strong sense of fantasy. Through the Colonel, the narrator evokes the past, and the Colonel's father, José Arcadio Buendía, the Colonel's mother, Úrsula Iguarán, the gypsy Melquíades, and the small band of settlers who founded the tiny village of Macondo.

Macondo is described as a place on no map; in fact, it is more a direction than a location. It is so rooted in the past, where time has stood still, that the town has a prehistoric atmosphere. Note that the "town" bears a close resemblance to the "memory" of a dream, for only in memory does time not move, and only in a dream – when a dream is remembered – is someplace really *no place*.

In Macondo, there is, seemingly, magic in everything. And solitude pervades and permeates everything. The town is described as lying outside civilization, behind mountains that lead to the ancient city of Riohacha, a place that many, many years ago was home to the Buendía ancestors. Riohacha is renowned as the object of an attack by Sir Francis Drake. This fabulous incident is the catalyst behind the Buendías' fear of incest, and "escaping" from Riohacha is necessary for the founding of Macondo.

The author then narrates the fable-like beginnings of Macondo by recreating scenes from the past. We are experiencing, as it were, a story foretold. When we finish the novel, the final Buendía to reach manhood will realize that Melquíades' manuscripts, written in code and Sanskrit, tell the history – in advance – of the Buendía family, its fortunes, and its collapse. For the present, however, we must listen to hints from the narrator, subtle clues in the narration, and realize that there is a doomed sensitivity within each Buendía, of which each is unaware. Thus, we begin, ironically, with Macondo's being founded as a sort of new Eden. Physically, it resembles Eden, and its patriarch,

José Arcadio I, is strong and confident that it will flourish. He is imbued with a sense of destiny, however, that, after one hundred years, it will end in oblivion. He dreams of a town with mirrors for walls; thus he begins the trek that leads to the town's initial site. A mysterious "voice" commands him to found Macondo on one particular site. Already, ordinary relations between things become scrambled and produce an improbable, yet a marvelous sense of magical reality. On the way through the jungle, for example, the pioneers discover an old Spanish galleon adorned with orchids and "smelling of solitude and oblivion." The ship has set rotting in a jungle clearing for centuries, and we are told by the narrator that the ship is the same one which Colonel Aureliano Buendía will discover years later during the long series of civil wars that he commanders. The settlers' encounter with the ship foreshadows the apocalyptic fate of the Colonel and provides the first section with dramatic momentum.

Macondo, with its Eden-like isolation, is a place of solitude. Yet the town-to-be has beckoned the settlers to its extreme isolation. Macondo's remoteness is described in the mytho-poetic language of the book of Genesis, and García Márquez' language evokes primitive yearnings. Macondo, however, is less a paradise than a limbo. That is, the settlers become so much of the town's raw, pre-human nature that they suffer a psycho-cultural condition in which they are not modern men, nor are they savages. They are simply, uniquely "different," suspended in time. Common things become lost because the names describing their use are forgotten. Things from the civilized world or past history have either been forgotten or are deemed so new that it becomes necessary to point, because things have not yet received a name. We may consider this observation a wry and perhaps fanciful one; but, upon reflection, we would have to concede that our lives are, in fact, full of encounters with things for which we lack identifying names— things, which to describe, it becomes necessary "to point."

The gypsy Melquíades brings inventions to Macondo, such as magnets and a magnifying glass the size of a drum. Later, other gypsies will bring "sewing machines that reduce fevers" and, finally, they will bring the world's largest, most glittering, "hot" diamond: ice.

In addition, the gypsy Melquíades gives the patriarch, José Arcadio I, a Sanskrit manuscript of which we spoke earlier. This gypsy will spark the patriarch with the ambition to acquire knowledge and power. Meliquíades, however, is a benign wizard rather than a Mephistopheles, but he does inspire José Arcadio I with the Faustian dream of leading

Macondo out of its limbo-like isolation. Such a goal requires the super-natural wisdom and power (so it would appear to the patriarch) that only the gypsies possess. Indeed, one of the gypsy tribes is reported to have been wiped off the face of the earth for having transcended all knowledge. That report will later prove ambiguous and fantastic, as will the report of the first "death" of Melquíades. Everything seems ambiguous; the tone of the narrator is hesitant, reluctant yet always convincing. There is a kind of facetious, sardonic quality to the fantasy, as well as to the humor. When Melquíades is reported dead, the author describes the gypsy as being devoured by squid. How would the narrator know about the squid? But the point of telling how Melquíades dies is mocking and funny. More important, the gypsy's demise exposes his apprentice, José Arcadio I, to the other gypsies' bedeviling sorcery.

Fear is a constant leitmotif, or theme, in the novel, and fear of incest provides an impetus for the peculiar Buendía travail. The chain of events begins in Úrsula Iguarán's fear of sexual relations with her husband, José Arcadio Buendía. Their families had intermarried for centuries, and one such union had produced a child with a pig's tail. After her own marriage, therefore, Úrsula is gripped with fear of producing another monster, and so she refuses to consummate her marriage. On one level, she exhibits irrational hysteria, providing another instance of the author's humor; for example, she wears a chastity belt with a thick iron padlock. On the other hand, the results of incest and in-breeding are well-known and feared—in even the most primitive human societies. But it is important to realize that the reason why the Buendías have been practicing incest for centuries is because of their *isolation*. They have been trapped in solitude for a very long time, and this condition becomes even more characteristic of their lives in Macondo. The likelihood of incest is therefore more probable than in civilized, more populous communities because social isolation makes incestuous affinity inevitable. The loneliness of the Buendías makes it ultimately impossible for them to share their affection with anyone from the outside. People like the pianola expert, Pietro Crespi, are always strangers and are easily rejected—especially for romantic involvement with a member of the Buendía family.

This kind of intense inter-familial affection literally consumes the entire family's attention. In the end, such incestuous energy diverts the family from the task of self-preservation. Incest becomes claustrophobia, a means of compelling the family to remain together forever or to, finally, return to the fold.

There is an incredible tone to the narrative as the outlandish facts of the Buendía genealogy unfold. The first Buendía-Iguarán coupling was related to Sir Francis Drake's attack on Riohacha. Generations later, the grandmother still feared similar assaults; so the family moved to a village where the Buendías lived. There begins the incestuous unions that resulted in a Buendía being born with a pig's tail. Centuries later, Úrsula Iguarán still fears such a child. But her chastity belt makes her husband the butt of local jokes concerning his manhood. Following a cockfight, the sullen loser, Prudencio Aguilar, makes a humiliating insult to Úrsula's husband. That insult prompts the Buendía patriarch to thrust his spear through Aguilar's throat. There is a grim, Freudian whimsy to the killing, and yet the incident is one of incredible violence. Part of the horror is relieved by the robust humor with which García Márquez narrates the ritualistic way that José Arcadio I handles spear. Following the murder, José and Úrsula at last consummate their marriage.

The "ghost" of Prudencio Aguilar continues to suffer from the spear wound in his throat, and he comes to haunt the Buendía household. Úrsula oftentimes sees him desperately trying to close his wound with "a plug of esparto grass." Or else, she finds him wandering through the house, looking for a glass of water. Aguilar's ghost becomes an intolerable presence, and yet his ghost becomes an extension of the couple's psychological guilts and fears. In his nineteenth-century masterpiece, *Thérèse Raquin*, French novelist Emile Zola has the dead husband of an adulterous wife appear as the macabre form of guilt so as to haunt both wife *and* lover. The use of a "ghost" in *One Hundred Years*, however, is not tragic. It is comic. The humor of Aguilar's ghost appearing suggests something very much like the absurd humor of the film *The Rocky Horror Motion Picture Show* or Mel Brooks' *Young Frankenstein*. Yet the ghost is, in a sense, somewhat terrifying to the Buendías. One night, for example, the couple cannot endure the appearance of the apparition any longer, and so they flee. Thus they begin the trek that leads to the founding of Macondo.

José Arcadio II is born on the expedition through the jungle. Presumably, he was conceived the night Aguilar was killed, when José Arcadio I literally raped his wife because of her accursed chastity belt. The narrator, however, never delves into the motive behind Úrsula's concession to her husband. She simply submits to his masculine passion and to the brutal yet comic expression of Latin machismo. At this point, the plot takes a significant new direction. José Arcadio dreams of a city with walls of "mirrors." In a scene reminiscent of

Moses' receiving the Ten Commandments, a "voice in the wilderness" commands José Arcadio I to found Macondo on one specific plot of ground. There, the town springs up, and, immediately, it sinks into isolation. José Arcadio II's birth is followed by the birth of Aureliano, who will become the Colonel. (Amaranta is born later.) Until the arrival of the gypsies, there is merely a primitive tribal kind of existence. As in Faulkner's mythical county of Yoknapatawpha, not much happens in Macondo. The atmosphere suggests rote and repetitious occurrences in the same actions, the same faces, and even in the same names for members of the same family. Relations are fraught with incestuous overtones; sexual energy, rather than love, permeates the fabric of social consciousness, and sex gives the relations between the Buendías a static electric quality, so much so that sparks seem ready to fly at any time.

A number of narrative spirals from the central plot theme begin to emerge. To the horror of his mother, José Arcadio II and the fortune-teller and housekeeper, Pilar Ternera, begin an affair. Úrsula's intervention causes José Arcadio II to flee with the departing gypsies. Then suddenly Úrsula leaves in search of her son, and she does not return for six months. When she does return, she is without her son. Instead, she brings with her a group of professional people who hasten Macondo's step into the twentieth century, into a future filled with "material progress."

Pilar Ternera bears José Arcadio II a son, José Arcadio— nicknamed "Arcadio." The child, however, is raised by his grandparents, something which indicates both family loyalty and its unresolved conflicts with machismo. In this case, the Buendía family accepts without fanfare or rancor the excesses of this son, who developed an enormous, monstrously virile penis during puberty. Pilar Ternera, in turn, then fulfills a similar need with José Arcadio II's lonely brother Aureliano (later, to be the Colonel). And not long after bearing José Arcadio II a son ("Arcadio"), she gives birth to Aureliano's son: a boy who is named Aureliano José.

The fantastic comic images that have until now seemed merely rhetorical become more elaborate and integral to the novel's fable-like narrative. A Guajiro Indian, Visitación, arrives in Macondo, fleeing her town's plague of insomnia and amnesia. Shortly thereafter, this sickness enters Macondo when the mysterious Rebeca arrives in town. We are told then that as a toddler, Aureliano had clairvoyant powers: he predicted that a cooking pot of his mother's would fall—just before it actually did. Now he foresees the arrival of his "step-sister," Rebeca, who will bring the plague to Macondo. As the villagers begin to forget the names of things and as they begin to suffer acute insomnia, the illness becomes a metaphor for lost innocence and pre-consciousness. Macondo has not emerged from its primitive state. Instead, the insomnia plague has made the town regress to the level of fetal consciousness, awake yet unable to articulate conscious impressions. For as the names of things and the names of the things' functions are lost, language itself atrophies, and human consciousness sinks into animal-like mindlessness. Then – as if by magic – a "resurrected" Melquíades appears – with a cure for the insomnia plague. Until then, the patriarch of the Buendía clan, José Arcadio I, had been fruitlessly trying to preserve the names of things with a dictionary-like computer, succeeding in making 14,000 entries.

Readers of García Márquez' other fiction will note the reappearance of names and types of characters from his earlier stories and novellas. Notable are the singer Francisco the Man (who defeated the devil in a story centering on a duel of improvisation) and "Catarino's store" (from the short story "The Sea of Lost Time"), Macondo's first mayor (the Magistrate), Don Apolinar Moscote, and, later, the priests Fathers Isabel and Nicanor (from the story "The Evil Hour"). The use of stock *types* is in keeping with the South American storytelling tradition, the *cuento*, in which a group of authors re-tell the same story to see which one of them can tell it with *the most exaggerated detail and humor*. Some critics see this tradition as being a key factor in modern European and South American literature. If one reads *Labyrinths* by the French author Alain Robbe-Grillet, one can understand how this tradition can seem modern and yet foreign to most contemporary American writers.

García Márquez is very much a new, innovative voice in literature. He is not merely *another* South American writer. He seems to have read all of the major writers of the last eighty years – as well as being familiar with the traditions of all Greek-fostered Western literature. Like the Irish writer James Joyce, García Márquez uses – sometimes to masterful excess – the full panoply of lyrical language and literary tricks available. In *One Hundred Years*, García Márquez even borrows characters that appear in someone else's fiction – namely, the Mexican revolutionary Lorenzo Galiván, borrowed from the novel *The Death of Artemio Cruz* by Carlos Fuentes.

   With the arrival of the self-proclaimed Mayor, Don Apolinar
Moscote, in Macondo, the town comes of political age. Moscote is
a Conservative politician, and he orders that all of the houses in
Macondo must be painted blue. That edict lays the seed of civil strife
and initiates the makings of the heroic exploits of the future Colonel
Aureliano Buendía. But first, Aureliano becomes wildly infatuated
with the Mayor's youngest daughter, the pre-adolescent Remedios.
García Márquez uses this anguished love affair to satirize the early
sexual promiscuity imposed on many young females in many Latin
American countries. Remedios is described as being so young that
she still wets the bed. Her betrothed is, in contrast, a reflection of
exaggerated, yet gentle, machismo. For while manhood in many South
American countries presupposes sexual vigor in the man, machismo
ties male promiscuity to virginity in the "macho" male's sexual part-
ner. In any country where sexual promiscuity is lauded in the male
but condemned in the female, virginity must be exalted beyond any
notions of common sense. For this reason, the "love child" and the
chiquita (the common-law wife) are found to be the rule in many South
American countries. With that in mind, we should find nothing ex-
ceptional about illegitimacy in One Hundred Years. But the mysterious
appearance of Rebeca and her subsequent adoption by the Buendías
are merely the author's sardonic view of this phenomenon.
   Once the insomnia and amnesia plague has been cured, Macondo begins to prosper. The town receives mail service, and there is
traffic between Macondo and other parts of the country. Commerce
begins, and Úrsula engages Pietro Crespi, an Italian pianola expert,
to teach the girls Rebeca and Amaranta to dance. The Buendías begin
to have bourgeois aspirations. Yet one notices, at the same time, that
Macondo is a town without an economy; it is an agricultural
community.
   Like so many third-world countries, the town must purchase
foreign, manufactured goods with its raw materials. Even experts like
Pietro Crespi are foreigners, and so services, as well as products, must
be imported. Macondo emerges, then, as a kind of metaphor for South
America and its relations with such developed countries as the United
States. There is a great desire for progress in Macondo, but there are
only natural resources to pay for that demand. In the final analysis,
the imported technology and manufactured goods that Úrsula's
strangers bring are more expensive than the natural resources

that the Macondians trade in exchange. Like the inventions that Melquíades introduces to the town, the fantastic technology of progress remains more curious than useful. And the knowledge to produce such wonderful things constantly eludes the Macondians themselves.

Macondo slowly moves out of its fantastic isolation. It slowly is invaded by foreigners—Yankees, government officials, Arab merchants, and brutal troops. In this report, Macondo may be regarded as a microcosm of South America's history. It is a fecund, yet a doomed Garden of Paradise, which loses its magical innocence to alien values, governmental idiocy, Yankee imperialism, inflated machismo, and human greed. Ultimately, Macondo is the apotheosis of the South American personality, the colonial child become liberated man.

For the most part, the subplots in this first section concern romance. Rebeca and Amaranta become obsessed with the Italian pianola expert. The unlikely romance between Aureliano and Remedios Moscote blossoms. Amaranta and Rebeca begin a violent rivalry for the affection of Pietro Crespi. These romances all have a comic touch to them. Out of despair, Amaranta mutilates her hand on a burning coal. Meanwhile, Pilar Ternera announces that she is pregnant with Aureliano's child. These developments all have a Rabelaisian color of hysterical comedy: love is interwoven with farce. All of the characters here are creatures of passion and all seemingly lack a social conscience. On the other hand, sexual appetite seems all-important. Aureliano Buendía, for instance, has been carrying his desire for Pilar Ternera since infancy in the "inviolable backwater of his heart." Rebeca consoles herself over the loss of Pietro Crespi by eating handfuls of dirt, leaving "a harsh aftertaste in her mouth and a sediment of peace in her heart." This vital sensuality is aided by unusually brilliant images and a language that heightens our levels of awareness. At the end of Section 4, we see the demise of the patriarch. José Arcadio Buendía goes mad, haunted by the ghost of Prudencio Aguilar. This sets the stage for the emergence of the Colonel: José Arcadio I's son—Aureliano.

SECTIONS 5 – 9

In some degree, tragedy is the fate of all the Buendías. Aureliano marries Remedios, but his happiness is cut short when she dies after her unborn twins become twisted in her womb. The patriarch becomes senile. He now "sees" Prudencio Aguilar so vividly that the ghost becomes a real person. Úrsula has her husband tied to a tree. Fantasy impinges so strongly on reality that the Buendías try valiantly but fail to restrain the patriarch's imagination. This melancholy turn of events is relieved by sharp religious satire. Father Nicanor Reyna, the town's first priest, attempts *to prove* the existence of God to the people of Macondo by drinking a cup of hot chocolate and then levitating. Pilar Ternera, a strange fortune-teller, gives birth to Aureliano José; Macondo is a fertile place. And the females are noted for their fecundity. But until José Arcadio II returns from his sudden sojourn, sexual conduct seems to follow the conventional patterns of a small town. José Arcadio II changes all of that. He introduces Macondo to a flagrant promiscuity, offering himself as a stud to the town's females.

Section 5 is a pivotal one. Here, the influence of the terrorist and medical quack, Dr. Alirio Noguera, combines his lust for subversion with the election fraud of Mayor Moscote to trigger the rebellious career of Colonel Aureliano Buendía. From this point on, the novel reaches beyond being a mere tableau of characters. The plot extends now into political symbolism and man's fate.

Colonel Aureliano Buendía begins his bloody odyssey. Hitherto, he has been apolitical. But the rigged election in favor of the Conservatives causes him to support the Liberal rebellion. He has neither political nor military background; he simply designates himself as "Colonel." Ostensibly, he struggles to rid the country of the political corruption and despotism of the Conservatives. Yet his goal is not entirely selfless. He leaves Macondo to the dictatorial rule of his brother, the huge José Arcadio II. Ultimately, the Colonel's violent avocation leads to disillusionment and cynical despair.

José Arcadio II seduces Rebeca. The pianola expert thus loses Rebeca and is haughtily refused by Amaranta. Doubly crushed, he becomes inconsolable and kills himself. So the incestuous ties of the Buendías again entangle another generation. But comic relief is never far away. A maturing Arcadio (III) is still unaware that Pilar Ternera is his mother, and, filled with an irresistible obsession for her, he tries to seduce her. We are treated to a farce reminiscent of Fielding's *Tom Jones*. There is the burlesque action of musical beds. But whereas Fielding's hero believed that he *had* slept with his mother, Arcadio (III) is cheated of this fate. Pilar Ternera arranges to have Sofía de la Piedad meet the boy in the darkness of night instead. Again, throughout these couplings, there is passion, but rarely love. Another curious note is that the relations between the sexes are absent of physical abuse. Clearly, the males dominate the Buendía household, but their authority is a dark, latent potential. They never display actual physical cruelty to the women. Male dominance is taken for granted, and the basis for it is merely suggested. García Márquez leaves the means of male authority to our imagination.

The Colonel's military revolt continues as his disillusionment and cynicism deepens. He finally concludes that the only difference between the Liberals and the Conservatives is the different hours that each faction attends mass. Worse, he determines that his heroic struggle has simply been another Latin American power play. In reality, he has been fighting the Conservatives only to see who will become *caudillo*—the country's "maximum man" or "jefe," as many South American strongmen are called. His isolation assumes preposterous dimensions, verging on suspicion, paranoia, and delusions of grandeur. As protection from would-be assassins, he sleeps inside a (literal) chalk circle. His heroic quest thus becomes absurdly sad. A mysterious gunshot kills the Colonel's brother, José Arcadio II. The murder scene becomes the occasion for García Márquez to demonstrate his great powers of lyrical, fantastic description:

> A trickle of blood came out under the door, crossed the living room, went out into the street, continued on in a straight line across the uneven terraces, went down steps and climbed over curbs, passed along the street of the Turks, turned a corner to the right and another to the left, made a right and another to the left, made a right angle at the Buendía house, went in under the closed door, crossed through the parlor, hugging the walls so as not to stain the rugs, went on to the other living room, made a wide curve to avoid the dining room table, went along the porch with the begonias, and passed without being seen under Amaranta's chair as she gave an arithmetic lesson to Aureliano José; and went through the pantry and came out in the kitchen, where Úrsula [José Arcadio II's mother] was getting ready to crack

thirty-six eggs to make bread.
"Holy Mother of God!" Úrsula shouted.

Following José Arcadio II's death, the patriarch himself dies. But the latter's death provides a striking mixture of pathos and comic, black humor. Over the years, the only person whom the patriarch has had any contact with is the ghost of Prudencio Aguilar. "They talked about fighting cocks. They promised each other to set up a breeding farm for magnificent birds, not so much to enjoy their victories which they would not need then, as to have something to do on the tedious Sundays of death." José Arcadio I's death is foretold by Cataure, Visitación's brother: "I have come for the exequies of the king." This improbable epitaph is followed by fabulous occurrences. Yellow flowers rain from the sky, carpeting the town, and smothering the animals sleeping outdoors. This pathetic end is relieved by the birth of twins to Santa Sofía de la Piedad: José Arcadio IV Segundo and Aureliano Segundo exemplify a regeneration of the Buendía male line.

With the conclusion of the civil war, Amaranta rejects the suit of the Colonel's best friend, Colonel Gerineldo Márquez. Her rejection adds to the triviality of the military struggle, in many ways symbolizing the war's sterility. She accuses Márquez of wanting to marry her *only* because he can't marry her brother, the Colonel. She declares that she will never marry anyone. This bleak panorama of the Buendía decline is then briefly enlivened by flirtations between young Aureliano José and his aunt Amaranta. Organized religion is then satirized when Father Nicanor's replacement, Father Coronel ("The Pup"), appears. And in another spiral off the main plot, seventeen illegitimate sons of the Colonel arrive, one by one, at the Buendía house. The young males are of all colors and races, and each has an indelible "look of solitude that left no doubt as to the relationship."

The effect of these episodes is maddeningly comic. The narrative hyperbole reveals deft touches of ironic wit, and we find some of the novel's best dramatic moments here. A benevolent Conservative general takes over Macondo and befriends the Colonel. When the Colonel re-takes the town, he has the general executed. Killing this authoritarian yet very humane character creates a scene of tragicomedy and fatalism. Murder, after all, is murder, and this killing is unwarranted. That incident signals the Colonel's own corruption into a true despot.

Thus, we see clearly that power corrupts and absolute power corrupts absolutely – an observation made by the political writer Lord Acton, and, Lord Acton added, most great men are nearly always *bad* men. The Colonel resembles no tragic tyrant so much as he resembles Shakespeare's Hamlet. Power has gripped the Colonel, distorting his idealism into a feeble caricature of such noble aspirations as justice and forbearance. Instead, we see a suspicious warlord, greedy for power, increasingly corrupted by weaker principles and having fewer and fewer scruples about using power. For example, he orders his friend Gerineldo Márquez executed because of a trivial matter. Only Úrsula's intervention saves Márquez at the last moment. But that incident shows the Colonel as a character condemned by his incapacity to love, or trust. His world is a singular one of potential rivals, where solitude, pain and disappointment are expected out of every relationship – a world where such morose afflictions of the spirit are self-fulfilling prophecies. In the end, the Colonel's fate is tragicomedy, a life of adventures capped by hilarity and laced with absurd ambiguity. After signing the Armistice Treaty of Neerlandia, which ends the civil war in a Conservative victory, he tries to kill himself. Earlier, Pilar Ternera had advised him to watch out for his mouth, so he aims the gun to his chest. But the bullet misses all his vital organs. At such ironic moments, the Colonel's life becomes more ambiguous, exuberant, and ludicrous. One day he is denounced for surrendering to the government. The next day, he is hailed as a hero and awarded the Order of Merit, which he rejects. And yet, all the perils that he has survived only seem to prepare him for oblivion. He retires to make and remake melted-down gold fish. His occupation is circular, repetitious, rote, and absurd; in fact, his life comes to resemble the plot that delineates his fate.

SECTIONS 10 – 12

The next generation of Buendías moves to the center of the action. Aureliano Segundo and Fernanda del Carpio are married and have a son, José Arcadio V. Úrsula nurses the wild fantasy that the young boy will someday become Pope. Her preposterous whim shows us a stark disproportion between false hopes and realistic plans. Her hope to send the child to Rome and, later, see him assume the papacy is a form of madness based on pride. Of course, the Segundo twins have their own delusions. They reflect cyclical lives and mirror the fates of the Colonel and his brother José Arcadio II. As the latter two brothers shared Pilar Ternera, so the Segundo twins sleep with Petra Cotes. "A panther-faced woman," Petra Cotes is delineated in the language of hyperbole and exaggerated sexuality. But she is more than simply fecund; her fertility is magical; and like Macondo's own regenerative powers, her fertility lacks practical control. She is described as generating wealth merely by riding around Aureliano's fields. Petra Cotes makes Aureliano wealthy, in the course of which she infuriates his wife. So formidable is her bounty that Aureliano is reduced to nonsensical babble: "Cease, cows, for life is short."

The tone of high comedy here marks García Márquez as a skillful practitioner of black humor. And we see this attitude in the author's treatment of Aureliano's wife. For all her beauty, Fernanda del Carpio has grotesque pretensions. An unbearable snob, she represents the straitlaced, hypocritical atmosphere of bourgeois conventions and their inevitable contradictions. She first appears as the intruding Queen of Madagascar. There is a suggestion (never proven, however) that her retinue includes the soldiers who carry out the massacre at Macondo's carnival. But she herself has to be rescued when the shooting starts. So her complicity seems remote and is largely ambiguous. During the massacre, Aureliano Segundo takes her to safety and falls in love with her.

Fernanda's cumbersome moral pretensions drive Aureliano back to Petra Cotes time and time again. If we may define black humor here as a droll indulgence in someone's self-inflicted folly, then Fernanda becomes the perfect vehicle for this kind of mirth. She refuses to defecate in anything but a golden, crested chamberpot, and she is described as suffering from a uterine disorder, but is too modest to see a doctor in person. Instead, she begins a long correspondence with an invisible doctor who prescribes a "telepathic operation." At the appointed time, she lies down and falls asleep. When she wakes, she has been stitched from her groin to her sternum. Madness and superstition become interwoven. Fernanda seems hellbent in driving her dignity into a false, destructive pride.

In other developments, we see the differing characters of the Segundo twins. While Aureliano is withdrawn, José Arcadio IV seems marked with a tragic sign. The latter experiences death and bestiality at an early age; he is said to have mastered black magic, and he introduces the town to its first water transportation—of a fantastic sort:

a log raft, pulled by thick ropes by twenty men, carrying a rich group of matrons is hauled through the jungle. In short, José Arcadio IV is outgoing, yet morbid, whereas Aureliano is cautious yet curious. As the novel unfolds, a number of sub-plots achieve their unity of effect. Sixteen of the Colonel's bastard sons are all executed one night. They are found shot through the indelible crosses of pre-Lenten ashes on their foreheads. Two of the sons were responsible for bringing the first train to Macondo, a yellow train resembling a "kitchen dragging a village behind it." The railroad opens Macondo up to Yankee imperialism. The train service also brings modern technology with all its ability to remove "where the limits of reality lay."

Macondo assumes the hustle and bustle of a boom town. Bruno Crespi, the brother of the dead pianola expert, Pietro Crespi, introduces a cinema into Macondo, and it is met by disbelief. The townspeople cannot understand how an actor dies in one film and reappears again in another. For all of the humor and nonsense, albeit highly imaginative nonsense, preceding this development, however, we now enter into the novel's tragic, somber phase. Two Yankees, Mr. Herbert and Mr. Jack Brown, arrive in Macondo to set up a banana company. Macondo's history is now presented to us as a vast synthesis of all the socio-economic evils that have plagued the southern hemisphere. But the novel's tempered concerns are *only in a symbolic sense*, historical. There are no dates nor chronology. Fantasy, moreover, confounds any real sense of linear time. There is a compelling logic to events that defies true chronology. For example, it is "only logical" that the indelible crosses on the Colonel's bastard sons will predestine their deaths. Thus, the absence of a historical linear time span enables the creation of fictional *reality* – the bastards will die forever in the same way for each reader.

Satire is never absent in the fiction of García Márquez. As an example, Remedios the Beauty is described in terms that make her resemble the Virgin Mary. Her beauty is the stuff of legends. Yet she causes the bloody deaths of at least four men before she herself ascends to heaven in waving folds of Fernanda's "brabant sheets." Such details are exaggerated as much for scorn as for ironic effect.

SECTIONS 13 – 14

Macondo prospers with the rise of the banana company and increased commerce. The Buendías settle into decline. Their household suffers increasing disruption and alienation from the town. Úrsula loses her eyesight, but she heroically compensates for its loss with her uncanny memory and sense of hearing. José Arcadio V is sent off to a seminary in Rome. (Remember that Úrsula believes that he can, and will, be Pope someday.) Aureliano Segundo moves in with Petra Cotes. A decadent materialism pervades the rest of the town; and perhaps it is best symbolized in the eating contest between Aureliano Segundo and the bestial director of a school of voice, a woman called Camila Sagastume, "The Elephant." The eating contest serves as a parody of machismo and also as an example of supreme irony, since in an effort not to lose a contest *to a woman*, Aureliano almost kills himself by overeating, and *does* lose the contest. Fernanda sends Meme away, trying to conceal Aureliano's affair with Petra Cotes from Meme. But this only increases Fernanda's moral discomfort rather than ameliorate her sense of shame or loss. She succumbs to hysterical self-deceptions and a *singing* rage that lasts for two days. Solitude so pervades the life of the Colonel at this point that he dies, his forehead pulled in between his shoulders, like a baby chick, leaning against the chestnut tree that harbored old José Arcadio I, the Colonel's father. Fernanda, like the Colonel, is an alienated creature: she suffers the humiliation of infidelity, while the Colonel collapses from the futility of making and melting down gold fish.

The Colonel's death is typical of the novel's alternative rhythms and moods. But his death is also the signal for a major farce.

Meme returns from boarding school accompanied by four nuns and her entire class of sixty-eight girls. The Buendía household is thrown into chaos. Fernanda has to order seventy-two chamber pots to alleviate the nocturnal congestion in the bathroom. The author's hyperbole is punctuated by sharp drama: when Amaranta is salting the soup, one of the nuns asks Amaranta what ingredient she is adding to the soup, and she receives the reply: "Arsenic."

After graduating from the convent, Meme's education continues in the streets of Macondo, where contrary to village prejudice, she befriends Patricia Brown, the Yankee daughter of the banana company owner. Patricia Brown opens to Meme a world closed to many Latin American women. García Márquez makes the Anglo girl symbolize the independent, assertive cosmopolite, especially in her attitudes towards men. Meme takes up these modern, feminist, Protestant values. She throws discretion and class prejudices to the wind and begins an affair with the mechanic Mauricio Babilonia. Their liaison has an ominous consequence for the Buendía clan.

Tragedy is often saved from gross sentimentality by the author's profuse humor. When it seems that the aging Amaranta will never die, she is visited by Death and told to begin making her shroud. Like the proctor of a final exam, Death (a woman, dressed in blue, with long hair) instructs her to take all the time she needs, to make the pattern as fine and as complicated as she wants, because she will die when it is completed. She finishes her shroud, then announces that she "is sailing at dusk, carrying the mail of death." Such black humor seems to crop up in the unlikeliest places. As another example, a guard shoots Mauricio Babilonia trying to climb through the tiles and get into Meme's bathroom. Instead of making his sexual rendezvous, however, the hapless mechanic is wounded and paralyzed from the waist down. He dies of old age in solitude, ostracized as a chicken thief.

No apparent strategem eludes the author's satirical vision of the classic love tryst. Humor and hyperbole lend dramatic emphasis to commonplace events. And the ambiguous tragicomic effect is further enhanced by oxymoronic phrases. In her affair with Mauricio Babilonia, for instance, Meme is protected by the "innocent complicity" of her father, Aureliano Segundo. This buffoonery is also sharpened in descriptions of sexual passion. A frigid Fernanda rears little Amaranta Úrsula, while corresponding with invisible doctors and carrying pessaries in her petticoats for her sexual aches.

SECTION 15

In characteristic Buendía fashion, Meme's affair with Mauricio Babilonia leads to a child. In addition, the infection of Yankee progress has brought with it a strong sense of bourgeois scandal and shame. Fernanda takes the pregnant Meme off to a convent in Cracow. After the boy is born, the nuns in Cracow return him to the Buendía house. Fernanda is, of course, furious. The reader might now expect that Fernanda's intention to conceal the child's origins would stop here. But García Márquez imbues his characters with a manic, disarming pride. Lies and rationalizations serve to make their predicaments only more entertaining. Fernanda tells Santa Sofía de la Piedad that the boy was found in a basket floating among the bullrushes. This outlandish lie is expropriated from the biblical story of the discovery of Moses. But Santa Sofía accepts it without reservation.

The major action now centers around the strike at the banana company. Dissatisfied workers protest working conditions and low compensation. True to South American conditions, the workers are revolutionaries as well as disgruntled cogs within the system. Aureliano Segundo and Colonel Lorenzo Gavilán lead the strikers. In other works of fiction, this situation might be labeled social-protest drama, but the situation here achieves tremendous narrative force and symbolism in the language of García Márquez. The strike and massacre are recalled through the memory of a child. In the language of the child narrator, humor, fantasy, and parody underline the horrors of Yankee exploitation. The workers are protesting real injustices, but their abuse by the Yankee imperialists has been so blatant that their situation seems almost ludicrous. Foremost, the workers do not even receive wages. They are paid in company scrip, a currency that will buy *only* Virginia ham *sold in company commissaries*. There are *no* health benefits for the workers; all illnesses or injuries are treated with copper sulfate pills that the town children collect for bingo games. The company at first responds to the strikers' demands with humiliating concessions, but the response trivializes the protest objectives. Latrines, for instance, are one of the demands; the company agrees to issue them—but *only at Christmastime*. Finally, the factory owner "disappears" under a forged death certificate, and the courts determine that the workers are really self-employed and thus do not, as it were, "exist." In all this irony and fraud, there is pain so exaggerated that it almost loses any power to effect the reader's commiseration. Still, the effect of the massacre is brutal; the narrative is rendered in a language brilliant with metaphors and strong rhythms. José Arcadio IV Segundo regains consciousness after being struck down during the massacre. He finds himself lying amid thousands of corpses on a two-hundred car train. Yet when he returns to Macondo, he is assured by everyone that nothing has happened. He is incredulous and retires to the gypsy's (Melquíades') room. Traumatized and terrified, he reads Melquíades' manuscripts and eventually loses his mind; he sees the massacre finally as a kind of surrealistic dream: ". . . the panic became a dragon's tail . . . swirling about in a gigantic whirlwind that little by little was being reduced . . . cut off all around like an onion being peeled by the insatiable and methodical shears of the machine guns." Arcadio's function from then on is to pass on knowledge of the manuscript to young Aureliano Babilonia.

Slowly, José Arcadio IV Segundo dissolves from outside view in the
eerie atmosphere of the room.

SECTIONS 16 – 20

In retaliation for the threatening workers' strike, Mr. Brown, we
are told, "unleashed a torrential rain" that lasts for four years, eleven
months, and two days. In addition, the duration of the storm makes
the Yankees single-minded, irrational, and vengeful. The rains fill the
lustful glutton Aureliano Segundo "with the spongy serenity of a lack
of appetite." To all intents and purposes, the town and its inhabitants
are "peering over the precipice of uncertainty." When the rains stop,
Macondo is in ruins. Úrsula slips into complete solitude; by now she
is merely a plaything for little Amaranta Úrsula and Aureliano
Babilonia. The matriarch begins to live in the distant past, beyond
senility, an absurd creature for whom existence lacks all meaning.
Section 16 begins the novel's denouement. José Arcadio V returns from
Rome, defrocked and in disgrace. Úrsula dies of old age. Her life has
been a tribute to endurance and industry. But at her death, she is
a caricature of her former self, shriveled up like a raisin. The hyper-
manical and prideful, prudish Fernanda develops voodoo powers. Her
jealousy feeds murderous intentions. Formerly, she could tolerate
Aureliano's sexual infidelity, but now his lust has turned to love —
with Petra Cotes. For that betrayal, she tries to kill him by sticking
pins in his photograph. She is successful, but just before he dies,
Aureliano sends Amaranta Úrsula off to school in Brussels. So begins
another serial possibility in the character of Amaranta Úrsula.
Aureliano's death by voodoo, however, does not indicate the ferocious
homicidal passion directed at him. The brutality of his death is in-
dicated only when Santa Sofía cuts the throat of his corpse: he is sym-
bolically butchered. Here, we should recall that García Márquez is
well-known for his flair of choosing the dramatic moment to conclude
a plot; thus, as we recall, the fate of the twins is tied — so when
Aureliano dies, his brother José Arcadio IV falls dead in Melquíades'
room. They both fall victims to the ravages of time.

The pace of the narrative quickens. Rebeca dies, and the circle
of characters tightens, thus concentrating now on the focus of *action*.
There are many harbingers of dire things to come. Father Isabel claims
to have seen a monster, described as "the Wandering Jew." And indeed a winged monster is caught and killed. Then strange omens

appear, described in the manner of ancient Aztec and Oriental accounts of preludes to natural disasters. The priest loses his mind; he is replaced by Father Ángel after a tongue-in-cheek account of celibacy's tendency to induce sexual derangement. Borrowing from his novella *Leaf Storm*, at this point, García Márquez offers the phenomenon of birds again – this time, bursting through windows during the mid-day heat and dying inside houses. Luminous orange discs pass through the sky. It is as though we are about to witness an earthquake. Such bizarre occurrences give a magic aura to the town's decline and portend the novel's ominous conclusion.

Aureliano Babilonia takes up the study of the gypsy's manuscripts again. In this task, he fulfills the logical expectations generated at the beginning of the novel. José Arcadio V (whom Úrsula had hoped would become Pope) at first scorns him and restricts him to the study. But this harsh sentence only makes Aureliano transcend the needs of physical existence, and his isolation compels him to embrace the intensity of his solitary struggle to unravel the mysterious Sanskrit codes. Another plot coil is unraveled when the last of the Colonel's seventeen bastard sons emerges. His appearance is another example of the author's cruel black humor. The man is fleeing from unknown assassins and seeks sanctuary at the Buendías' house. The two men refuse to let the fugitive inside, and later he is murdered in the same way as his brothers – shot through the ashen cross on his forehead.

The relationship between José Arcadio V and Aureliano remains cool until Aureliano aids José Arcadio V during an asthma attack. We learn then something of José Arcadio V's debaucheries in Rome. His corruption had only been hinted at earlier. But now we see the extent of his depravity. He engages children in nightly orgies. His lascivious nature finds its penalty in the excesses of his partners, and after one wild party, the children drown him in his tub. It is one of the funniest, and most absurd, scenes in the novel.

A mature Amaranta Úrsula returns to Macondo. She is married to an older Flemish gentleman, Gaston, a madcap entrepreneur who owns (and rides) a strange velocipede. The history of the Buendía family emerges as a labyrinth within the chaos of history in these final chapters.

In a zoological brothel, Aureliano Babilonia meets Pilar Ternera, his great-great-grandmother, now an aged whore who mistakes him for the Colonel and reveals the crushing details of the youth's antecedents. Pilar Ternera, we realize, becomes aware of the completion of the final, temporal plot. Thus, she places Aureliano in touch with his origins and provides a mechanism for fulfilling the expectations generated in the first chapter sections.

Aureliano begins to try and decipher Melquíades' manuscript in earnest. His study becomes an obsession, relieved only by visits to the bookstore of the wise old Catalonian, his meetings with the four friends whom he meets there, and his visits to the black prostitute, Nigromanta. His obsession with learning assumes the energy of sexual passion, a vague but powerful life-force. It is an energy that also finds sexual expression in the form of passion for his aunt Amaranta. Gaston gives the adulterous pair his blessings, and they fulfill the ancient Buendía curse. Tragedy follows, and Aureliano loses both the child and Amaranta. The fate of the child is especially horrible, but we find his end preordained in the epigram of Melquíades: "The first of the line is tied to a tree and the last is being eaten by ants." As the last pages of the manuscript are about to be revealed, the single, remaining room of the old Buendía house is filled with voices of the past. Melquíades' manuscript then assumes the dimensions of a metaphor for the unity of time and place: just as Melquíades and Aureliano, as writer, reader, and translator, are merged into one ghostly voice, Macondo is swept away in a storm, So the fantastic story ends in the moment when obliteration eradicates the town, the Buendías, and the narrator.

CHARACTER ANALYSES

José Arcadio I Buendía

The Buendía males are all enterprising, passionate dreamers, but José Arcadio Buendía is at once the most notable and the most eccentric. Forever fascinated by the unknown, he is a man for whom no form of reality will ever live up to what he imagines can be further discovered. Hardly a mad scientist, he nonetheless takes up project after project, invention after invention, so as to arrive at the ultimate truth of life. This excessive zeal is a virtue, in that it enables him to discover Macondo, but it is also a form of madness.

José Arcadio Buendía takes the life of Prudencio Aguilar, in an argument over José Arcadio's impotence and Úrsula's virginity, and

José Arcadio can never forget his taunter, and the ghost eventually finds him. But for a long time, however, José Arcadio I lives the life of a man who has no memory or past, and in leaving the world, he achieves solitude by psychological regression. His fascination with familiar instruments indeed seems real because it comes as a consequence of his flight from a bad memory (indeed, all memory of the world as it is). His agent and friend, the gypsy Melquíades, is the purveyor of mundane, archaic things which feed his appetite for novelty. Through Melquíades and the gypsy band, José Arcadio I acquires a magnet to locate gold, a telescope to eliminate actual physical distance, an ancient camera to photograph God, and a player pianola, flying carpets, ice, and other wonderful "inventions." When José Arcadio I is not involved with some "new" invention, he builds bird cages to fill Macondo with bird songs, which incidentally enable the gypsies to always find the town.

José Arcadio Buendía flees the tranquility of his native village to found Macondo. This flight is born of personal pride and indignation, but from that beginning, violence becomes associated with every action in the novel, from the social violence of civil wars, political treachery and martyrdom, to the violence of inner anguish, self-abnegation and personal despair. Through suggestion and often vivid metaphorical description, García Márquez forces the reader into a state of expectation that life in Macondo is bound to a brutal end. The characters and the events alike are born of force (and not only in the sense of physical rape), and they pass away in collision with other brutal forces. José Arcadio II settles down into the role of feudal lord, having taken forcible possession of the best plots of land around Macondo and oppressively taxing local peasants. He becomes a kind of heroic tyrant, saving his brother from execution by firing squad only to close his bedroom door forever to the sound of gunshots. There is only the suggestion that José Arcadio II is shot to death; no wound is ever found on his corpse and no weapon is ever found. But his body reeks with the smell of gunpowder. Besides the physical sense of violence, the major characters all seem to have some uncontrollable proneness to cruelty or blind rage. José Arcadio II's son, after the departure of the Colonel, assumes responsibility for Macondo but the role makes him power-mad. Amaranta, sister of the Colonel, is so consumed by jealousy that her rage at Rebeca Buendía causes her to suffer massive attacks of fever; in the end, her passion leads her to disfigure herself. Thus violence, like the murdered ghost of Prudencio Aguilar, infuses the town and the Buendía household.

The endless quests of José Arcadio I recall to us the character of Don Quixote. Perhaps critic Jack Richardson described him best as a "spiritual conquistador." But if so, José Arcadio I is one who never conquers his spirit, nor satisfies his appetite for intellectual novelty. Eventually, of course, the patriarch's energy and fascinating sense of wonder become rote formulas. Although he fails to photograph God, he has a street in Macondo named *God Exists*. And when at last he realizes the world of pure imagination, where all things become ever more wonderful, he goes mad and spends his last years tied to a chestnut tree in his backyard. There, babbling in medieval Latin, he argues with the first priest in Macondo, Father Nicanor Reyna, against all the imagined proofs for the existence of God. When he dies, his ghost remains under the chestnut tree, and he is Úrsula's consolation, although invisible to everyone else, except when Colonel Aureliano Buendía, his son, almost commits suicide. At various points in the latter half of the novel, José Arcadio I reappears as he does that first time, "soaking wet and sad in the rain and much older than when he had died." In the house of his great granddaughter-in-law, Fernanda, he is the only *dead* ghost, in contrast to the three *live* ones — Amaranta sewing on her shroud, Úrsula utterly blind, and Colonel Aureliano Buendía defeated and alone with his metal goldfish. For all his lust and ebullience, José Arcadio I is painfully fragile.

Episodes 4 through 15 depict the rise and fall of Macondo as contact with civilization develops and as political, economic, and humanistic ideals become corrupted. Organized rebellion, political ideologies, and scientific inventions transform Macondo from a kind of idyllic paradise into a banana factory boom town. García Márquez recreates the social and historical life of a small Colombian town; and as with Faulkner's Yoknapatawpha County, the town reflects a universal human condition — whether it is a nameless place or Macondo. Here, Macondo is a place that has hazy contours and uncertain statistics, and vague demographical features make distance evaporate. It is indeed more than one place — with more than its share of small-town tedium and redundant experiences. It is a South American Jefferson, Mississippi, or Winesburg, Ohio. At other times, it is not even a hamlet — merely, in the author's words, "a solution of convenience," a town large enough to merit daily train service from the legislative capital. It is also a place having only one cinema, but at least two priests (Fathers Isabel, "the Pup," and Nicanor) whose tenures overlap, and half a dozen colonels suffering guilt and an asphyxiating solitude. What counts, however, is what the town evokes, not what it is—a place where ghosts from the troubled past re-enter the present, not for revenge but as re-directed characters, as epiphanies of the agonizing present (Prudencio Aguilar, for example).

The characters who populate Macondo are, like those in Faulkner's fictional South—misfits, defeated rebels, and madmen. They struggle on heroically, through attacks by bandits, plagues, droughts, floods, continual civil wars, and the increasing solitude of those who have lost historical moments or who have been defeated by fate. The novel uses many allusions to biblical stories in order to create sardonic situations and to effect mythical comparisons. We have already mentioned the Buendía trek that led to the founding of Macondo—its all too obvious parallel to the wanderings of the twelve tribes of Israel in their search for Canaan, mankind's paradise lost, the Promised Land. The birth of the last Buendía to reach adulthood, Aureliano Babilonia, will suggest the birth of a lost Moses in order to make the parallel even stronger. He enters the story as a baby "discovered in the swamp bullrushes." There are also indirect references to religious and social Jeremiahs, Messiahs, and even the Jewish Diaspora. This last historical and social allusion, in particular, is given direct representation in the character of the Wandering Jew.

The floods, the plagues, and the other disasters that Macondo suffers, the political martyrs, and the emergence of the town from a pristine Eden-like wilderness—all these provide specific examples of the author's allusions to the Bible and other scenes drawn from religious contexts. But more often than not, the use of religious myths is highly cynical. The Immaculate Assumption of the virginal Remedios (who ascends to heaven, wrapped in "brabant sheets") is, needless to say, a very obvious example of the author's profane sense of irreverence towards traditional Latin American religiosity. Many of the author's biblical allusions are this explicit, but some are merely evocative and loosely parallel to episodes from the Old Testament and Roman Catholic tradition. They all, however, evoke our memories of the great literature of Western tradition. The novel starts with a Genesis (Macondo) and leads us through floods, storms, plagues, wars, famine, and culminates in an Apocalypse. Macondo is thus a vision drawn from Adam and Eve's Paradise, where men and women have only the simplest needs and desires, no matter that such a race can sometimes be homicidal – as it is in the Bible. Their passions are pristine, aboriginal, and intense; and so their life excludes knowledge of evil. Macondo begins as a preconscious place where the moral sense of the people is fetal, without language and without distinctions of right and wrong. The village is a world of aboriginal memory; the residents have to invent a language for unknown (unknowable) things of contemporary life that already exist but which cannot come into the consciousness of Macondo (as well as the mind of the reader) until the things have been named, until the things have been given distinctive articulation from the nameless void of material everything (or nothing). "There are," wrote one astute critic, "[in *One Hundred Years of Solitude*] only *mystifications* wherein a dead past wants to pass for a live present and *mystifications* in which a live present also repossesses the life of the past." (Carlos Fuentes, "Cien Años de Soledad," *Siempre*, No. 679, June 29, 1966.)

In Macondo, religion is bizarre, if not altogether irrational madness. One of the parish priests ("The Pup") delivers sermons consisting of daily gleanings from the Bristol Almanac. In Macondo, weather reports have more relevance than sermons from the Scriptures. The predictable, in this mythical world, must be the unexpected; and when the unexpected is not sin, it is either satire or magic. The gypsy Melquíades, whose age is as immortal as the ancients of the Bible, wrote the history of the Buendías in anticipation of all the events narrated in the novel itself. He dies, but returns to life "because he is unable to bear loneliness." Here the narrator becomes God-like, and we have to accept the author's sense of fantasy, for in the person of Melquíades, the boundary separating reality from unreality goes to pieces. Anything can happen, and, if necessary, one may die and be returned to life or "take portraits of God Himself."

In the literature of the world – the real Macondo – the essential definitions of life have to wear a country's cultural clothes, so to speak, those that have been tailored in the artistic imagination. Thus myth and science alike are hostages to the artistic transformations of human languages, and through language, human understanding of the world, as it is and as it is not yet. To paraphrase Melquíades, words have a life of their own. In time, our most revered religious institutions are captive to stylistic change and artistic fancy of meaning.

Colonel Aureliano Buendía

The longest shadow in the novel is cast by José Arcadio's son Colonel Aureliano Buendía. As the most outstanding member of the second generation, so it is through his triumphs and failures that we
come to understand the theme of solitude. He fulfills the novel's re-
quirements of circular myth and lineal history. The opening sentence
of the first chapter invokes a mythical, as opposed to a lineal time,
so that the plot comes full circle later on: "Many years later, as he
faced the firing squad, Colonel Aureliano Buendía was to remember
that distant afternoon when his father took him to discover ice." In
that allusive beginning, the future and past of the novel are linked,
so that he is identified as the novel's most palpable presence, an absurd historical figure, with mythical qualities. But García Márquez
tricks us; the Colonel is *not* killed by a firing squad. He dies, finally,
in solitude, leaning against the same chestnut tree where his mad
father was tied for so many years. The Colonel, Aureliano Buendía,
is the first human being born in Macondo. We learn early that he
is already doomed to a kind of cyclical fate, in that as leader of the
revolutionary forces, he follows the same route from Macondo to
Riohacha, discovering the same Spanish galleon as had his father.
"Silent and withdrawn," his fetus "weeps" in Úrsula's womb. His eyes
are open at birth. Clairvoyant, he is possessed of prophetic powers;
he predicts the arrival of Rebeca, his adopted sister, as well as deaths
and common household catastrophes. People are inclined to relate
his prophetic talent to his having wept in Úrsula's womb, just as later,
his cousin Aureliano Segundo relates his drive for power to some kind
of instinctive fear. The truth comes to his mother, Úrsula, however,
just before his death; in fact, the fetal weeping and glorious dreams
meant only that he had "an incapacity for love." Before the truth and
his death, however, there is already legend, "simultaneous and con-
tradictory information." His affair with Pilar Ternera, who bears his
son Aureliano José, ends in tragic results, as does his ill-fated revolution. Already, however, he is stamped with a heroic genius.

As we have noted, we learn that adolescence made Aureliano silent
and "definitely solitary." His brooding demeanor strikes both an echo
and a foreboding in our minds of action that we know must soon occur.
He is always quiet and subdued. He apprehends future events intuitively but his gift of prophecy becomes the motive for all his later
misadventures. Rebeca (who wanders into Macondo, carrying the

bones of her family in a bag, eating dirt and scraps of whitewash) brings to Macondo the highly infectious plague of insomnia and amnesia. It is Aureliano Buendía, still a child, who strikes on the solution that enables the town to remember things until the plagues pass away. This episode marks him, serendipitously, with legendary powers.

The first mayor of Macondo, Don Apolinar Moscote, brings violence, conservative politics and beautiful daughters to Macondo. One of the girls, Remedios, is married to the Colonel when she is still so young that she still wets the bed, plays with dolls and has not yet had her first menstrual period. It is through the Colonel's friendship with Don Moscote that he is introduced to political election frauds and political terror. After witnessing his father-in-law's Conservative troops murder a woman, Aureliano calls his friends, Gerineldo Márquez and Magnífico Visbal, to launch a Liberal revolution.

Here the real saga of Colonel Aureliano Buendía begins. And with the Colonel's rise to leadership of the rebel forces, Macondo moves out of its isolation into political conflict. The cause that Colonel Aureliano serves is progressive but vague; and more often than not he appears to be more rebel than revolutionary ideologue. In fact, he might almost be characterized as a rebel without a cause. He organizes thirty-two armed uprisings and loses each and every civil war. Throughout, however, he seems motivated by some kind of insatiable rage which is either altogether a justification for his own cruelties or a delusion. We never know, since at the height of his power he becomes as ruthless as his Conservative oppressors. He is so ambiguous that even his would-be executioners mistake the intensity of his rage as praying. He escapes from death—through the intercessions of his brother, the brutal José Arcadio II—only so that he can sign the treaty of Neerlandia, an ignominious surrender which leads to the extermination of the Liberal forces. His military career has taken him through three phases which parallel the three civil wars between Liberals and Conservatives recorded in Colombian history. García Márquez' grandfather, in fact, served under the Liberal leader of the period, General Rafael Uribe. Though exaggerated for ironic effect, Colonel Aureliano Buendía's struggle is a reflection of true historic events. The novel's historical facts, however, become tragic myths within the context of this fantasy novel.

After surrendering to the government, the Colonel declines a pension and retires to his occupation of manufacturing little metal goldfishes and writing poetry. Later, when Macondo is subjected to the exploitation of an American-owned banana company, and when the government reneges on its promise of pensions to his former comrades, the Colonel is outraged and tries unsuccessfully to foment another rebellion. Once again, he is left to making gold fish but this time, the humiliation of defeat is no longer disguised. He dies, urinating in his backyard, alienated and alone in the solitude of other heroes whom their country has forgotten.

For awhile, the Colonel's presence continues in the form of a street that bears his name. His seventeen sons, after being indelibly stained with pre-Lenten ash crosses, are systematically shot through the forehead. The last to die, Aureliano Amador, manages to survive into the final scenes of the novel, but he too meets the same fate. The assassination of the Colonel's sons highlights the incredible survival capacity of the Colonel. He escapes fourteen attempts on his life, seventy-three ambushes, a firing squad, a lethal dose of strychnine, and attempted suicide. Unlike José Arcadio Buendía I, his father, who continues in the novel after death as a ghost whom only Úrsula sees, the Colonel fades away into memory. His presence is felt later, however, when we are told that the last adult Buendía, Aureliano Babilonia, physically resembles him; and he becomes, as it were, the Colonel when he steps into a zoological brothel operated by a madam, Pilar Ternera, who is one hundred and forty-five years old.

Aureliano's contemporary and friend, Gabríel Márquez, is the grandson of Colonel Gerineldo Márquez, and the latter also remembers the Colonel because of his own grandfather. By then, the street named after Colonel Aureliano Buendía has disappeared. Only one photograph was ever taken of him, the daguerreotype of the Buendías. The Colonel survives more as legend than history when the last Buendía dies and Macondo is swept away in a hurricane.

Earlier, at the death of the Colonel, Macondo had already been battered to the point of collapse. His heroism and grand compassion, in fact, have made no real difference to the town. His tragedy is that he was destined to cause the death and suffering of people whom he wanted most to save. Ultimately, his battles and even his existence have no meaning. By the end of the novel, the street which bears his name has disappeared. The only photograph ever taken of him —

the Buendía family daguerreotype—has also by then almost faded away. Thus his solitude becomes an almost retrospective future, a cyclical fate. Through his character there is the suggestion of an unresolved action that cannot be completed. He is charmed, as it were, against violent death, but not, as critic Michael Wood observed, dying (*Columbia Forum*, Summer, 1970, Vol. XIII, N. 2). When he dies, his memory is only just a memory. Nothing ends for any of the characters, in fact, except life itself. The Colonel lives on as a memory in the memories of Aureliano, his friend Gabríel Márquez, and Pilar Ternera.

The Colonel's mythical life serves as an escape from the inevitable harsh and tragic fate that he meets. But his saga renders an enduring spirit of adventure which pervades the Buendía clan, constantly invoked by recurring devices and patterns. Besides genealogy, there is repetitive memory, as witnessed in the same names—generation after generation. The José Arcadios are brash, impulsive and lusty; the Aurelianos are reclusive, lucid and solitary. The women are, like Úrsula, either strong and waspish, or like Remedios, frail and sensuous.

José Arcadio II

Conceived and born before the founding of Macondo, José Arcadio II is the oldest child of José Arcadio and Úrsula Buendía. If he has none of the imagination of his younger, swashbuckling brother, he nonetheless has passion and machismo equal to that of the Colonel. At the age of fourteen, his prodigious sexual development stirs Úrsula's latent fears of years past. For her, his over-sized sex organ seems as unnatural and as cursed as her cousin's reputed pig's tail. This fear of incest and genetic deformity gives the story a cyclical rhythm. Soon enough, the young José Arcadio II becomes the lover of Pilar Ternera, Macondo's fortune teller. He is attracted to her, so we are told, "by the smell of smoke" under her armpits and skin. This episode sustains the myth of Buendía original sin and is followed by a series of incestuous episodes: Amaranta and her nephew Aureliano José; Pilar Ternera and her son Arcadio; and Amaranta and her great-great-nephew José Arcadio V, who drowns in his bath, debauched and forlorn, still "thinking about Amaranta."

The affair between José Arcadio II and Pilar Ternera quickly bears predictable results. But Pilar Ternera's announcement that she has borne his child so frightens and depresses him that he runs away with a gypsy girl and her people, "a red cloth around his head." Úrsula flies from Macondo in search of her son. Returning five months later, she brings new settlers from civilization and they open the town to all the good and evil aspects of material progress. Meanwhile, the son of José Arcadio II and Pilar Ternera is born. He is called "Arcadio," although baptized as "José Arcadio," to avoid confusion. "Arcadio" is brought up not by his mother but by his grandparents, a situation which parallels the author's life.

When José Arcadio II returns to Macondo, he is a full-grown man. He has been around the world sixty-five times; he is a member of "a crew of sailors without a country." His massive physical stature and his fabulous tales of adventure—he has practiced anthrophagy, slain sea dragons and seen the ghost of the Caribbean pirate Victor Hugues—lure the women of Macondo in a manner reminiscent of Esteban, a character from García Márquez' short story "The Handsomest Drowned Man." After cutting a wide swath through the lovely women of Macondo, José Arcadio II displaces Pietro Crespi in the affection of his (José Arcadio's) step-sister Rebeca. After brutally breaking Pietro Crespi's engagement, José Arcadio II marries Rebeca. The union is legitimized—to the dismay of Úrsula—but Father Nicanor reveals in a Sunday sermon that the couple were not really brother and sister after all. Úrsula, nevertheless, forbids them to ever enter in the family house again.

Later, José Arcadio II moves into a home built by his son Arcadio and settles down into the role of feudal lord. He tries to take forcible possession of the best plots of land around Macondo and taxes peasants "every Saturday with his hunting dogs and his double-barreled shotgun" on the grounds that Macondo's land had been wrongly distributed by his mad father.

He becomes a kind of heroic tyrant in one dramatic episode when he is able to save his brother from execution by a firing squad. However his own death is violent yet ambiguous, with some reference to Rebeca's complicity (see parallels in García Márquez' short stories "Montiel's Widow" and "One Day After Saturday"). The author's narrative only *suggests* that José Arcadio was shot:

> As soon as José Arcadio closed the bedroom door the
> sound of a pistol shot echoed through the house. A

trickle of blood came out under the door, crossed,
the living room, went out into the street, continued
on in a straight line across the uneven terraces . . .
[until it reaches the family home].

There is no wound on his corpse and no weapon is ever found. But the body reeks strongly of the smell of gunpowder; the stench is so strong, in fact, that it continues rising from the grave until the banana company has to cover it with a shell of concrete.

Machismo is a quintessential trait of José Arcadio II. He needs to express his masculinity through brute force, sexual profligacy, proliferation of male heirs, and subjugation of others, especially women. Machismo is both responsible for his gallantry and for his courage, as well as his suicidal persistence in the face of certain failure. It also figures in his postering and his abundance of false pride.

Melquíades, the Gypsy

The most important presence in the novel outside of the major Buendía male and female characters is the gypsy Melquíades, whose manuscript turns out to be the narrative of the Buendías. He is the gypsy friend of José Arcadio Buendía I, and he introduces Macondo to a host of fabulous things – flying carpets, magnets, daguerreotypes, ice, telescopes, and so on. He appears at the very beginning of the book and reappears in various ghostly reappearances; he stays around until Aureliano Babilonia begins the task of completing the translation of the parchment manuscripts – which Melquíades gives to José Arcadio Buendía I. It is important to remember that Melquíades is merely the narrator of the manuscripts – the story itself (in the sense of García Márquez' use of history as sequential time and existence as a simultaneous time) is created by the reader and author together.

Melquíades is an irrepressible and fantastic spirit. Always superhuman or concerned with the supernatural, he survives numerous scourges and afflictions that would be fatal to ordinary mortals. After numerous false deaths, he reappears in Macondo to report that he "died of fever on the sands of Singapore" and not as falsely narrated earlier, because of a squid attack.

He is a heavy gypsy with a wild beard and "sparrow hands." All of his wonderful inventions can be summed up in his exclamation to José Arcadio Buendía I, when they are introduced for the first time: "Things have a life of their own." It is rumored that Melquíades possesses magical powers and the "keys of Nostradamus." He is supposedly knowledgeable in the ancient writings of the monk Herman the Cripple. In return for his wonderful inventions, José Arcadio I gives him a room to conduct his harebrained experiments, and "his knowledge reaches unbearable extremes." His forty tribes of gypsies, in fact, are said to have been "wiped off the face of the earth because they had gone beyond the limits of human knowledge."

After he dies, the first time, Melquíades returns to Macondo as a ghost (albeit an ambiguous one) "with a dazzling glow of joy" because, so we are told, he could not bear "the solitude of death." A composite of mythical and human elements, he is depicted as "a prodigious creature . . . enveloped in a sad aura, with an Asiatic look that seemed to know what there was on the other side of things." His knowledge is supra-human but he never laughs because scurvy has caused his teeth to drop out. Years after his "death," he returns to live with the Buendías in a room built especially for him. His second "death" appears to be a natural one. But although his body is buried, he remains in the home as a ghost in Colonel Aureliano's workshop. There, he spends hours on end scribbling his enigmatic literature on parchment sheets – in fact, the history and destiny, already mentioned, of the Buendías and Macondo. He also has time to entertain young Aureliano.

Long after "death" and burial, the ghost of Melquíades continues to be heard, shuffling through the rooms. Aureliano Segundo opens the door of the study a generation later to discover Melquíades "under forty years of age. He was wearing the same old-fashioned vest and the hat that looked like a raven's wings and across his pale temples, there flowed the grease from his head that had been melted by the heat, just as Aureliano and José Arcadio had seen him when they were children." He last appears to Aureliano Babilonia to give advice on which books to locate at the wise old Catalonian's bookstore in order to translate the parchment manuscript. Then he disappears.

Melquíades fulfills a dual function as narrator and mythical archetype. It is he who introduces knowledge to Macondo, by way of his inventions as well as with the stories of his adventures; and it is he who provides the linear historical thread of the town's progression. But the most important aspect of his character is that his manuscript is the novel that chronicles the origins and fates of the Buendías. Melquíades is the author of the story – written in Sanskrit, in a "Lacedeamonian military code," and in "the private cipher of the Emperor Augustus." In curing Macondo of insomnia, Melquíades takes the townsfolk away from Eden, as it were, into material progress and irreversible history.

Úrsula Buendía

In all the stories by García Márquez, the women have long lives. They seem more able than the men to make the best of life, and to finally accept the inevitable solitude of aging in chronological time. Jack Richardson, in his review of this novel, correctly summed up this difference: "When Colonel Buendía dies, one feels the poignancy in the death of a single being; but when Úrsula is buried, one understands that life itself can be worn down to nothing" (*The New York Review of Books*, March 26, 1970). But these stalwart bastions of adversity rarely seem to triumph over the machismo of the Buendía males. Indeed, the female Buendías put up with a multitude of suffering and, as a result, become insensitive to the self-degradation (or in Fernanda's case, hypocrisy) of their body-and-soul loyalty to their men. If the men are ruined by monomania, the women are reduced by their blind constancy. For instance, none of the women really strikes one as erotic although the book abounds with Rabelaisian couplings. But the sexual act is always a mechanical thing, something abstract despite or because of García Márquez' sexual rhetoric (for example, "cat howls in her stomach"; "a panther-faced woman in profile"). In *One Hundred Years of Solitude*, sexuality is muted in maternal desire, which not surprisingly expresses itself through incestuous relationships.

The pillar of the Buendías is Úrsula Buendía, the wife of Macondo's founder, José Arcadio Buendía. Like her husband, Úrsula comes from an early South American family, living in a sleepy coastal village. The Iguaráns and the Buendías have been mating for centuries, and despite the rumors circulating among the two families concerning genetic mutations (the birth of babies as armadillos, or born with pig's tails), Úrsula marries José Arcadio Buendía. After Macondo is founded, she becomes the mother of Aureliano (the Colonel), Amaranta, and José Arcadio, and she is mother to the adopted Rebeca.

When José Arcadio Buendía loses his mind, Úrsula ties him to a chestnut tree and keeps the family going. When her grandson Arcadio becomes dictator, she prevents him from executing Don Apolinar Moscote, the Mayor. She tries unsuccessfully to arrange a marriage between Amaranta and the Italian pianola expert, Pietro Crespi. Then she banishes José Arcadio II and Rebeca for what she considers an unnatural marriage, and she thinks that she will die of shame when her daughter, Amaranta, refuses to wed Pietro Crespi.

Úrsula is very much a part of Macondo's history, especially its linear chronicle; she is always in the thick of the action. After the capture of Colonel Aureliano Buendía, during the first rebellion, she smuggles a revolver to him in an attempt to help him escape. This strategy fails, although the Colonel is ultimately saved from execution by his brother. Through this period of the Buendía defeat, she becomes the "only human being who succeeds in penetrating" the Colonel's misery. Her powers of sympathetic insight even give her the power of prophecy; she foresees the death of her son José Arcadio II. But time and tragedy are cyclical for her — sadness and solitude are, in fact, where she expects to find them. She never loses her equanimity, however, when misfortune, flood, incest, death or disease occur, for Úrsula always knows that they will be "on time."

In addition, Úrsula is calm when the Colonel's seventeen bastard sons arrive at her house, and she shows no emotion when they are systematically executed. At heart, Úrsula is always loyal and tender, just as she is proud and principled. She hides the gold discovered in her house (in the plaster statue of St. Joseph), planning to return it to its rightful owner if he should ever return. Her children would gladly use this wealth; they need it, and she herself wants to finance José Arcadio V's education so that he can become Pope. But she made up her mind not to use the money when she hid the money, and she will not relent.

At the age of a hundred, Úrsula goes blind. She has memorized sounds, smells and distances, however, and by memorizing everything, she is able to disguise her affliction until well into the third generation; and she still has her keen insight into character. Only Úrsula recognized that the Colonel was driven to his reckless adventures by "fear"; only Úrsula really appreciates the quiet courage of Fernanda, and the seriousness of the incestuous nature of the relationship between Aureliano José and Amaranta, his aunt.

Slowly, Úrsula metamorphoses into a kind of gnarled, decrepit doll for the children's amusement. She shrinks into a timeless state, confusing the past for the present to such an extent that she believes that her great-grandmother, Petronila Iguarán, has once again died. The children, Aureliano and Amaranta Úrsula, participate in her confusion by describing the presence of imaginary relations long dead. Totally blind, Úrsula converses with these imaginary persons as if they were actually there. "She finally mixes up the past with the present in such a way that in the two or three waves of lucidity that she had before she died, no one knew for certain whether she was speaking about what she felt or what she remembered." Yet, she persists in doing household chores throughout (1) the rainstorm which was "unleashed" by Mr. Brown, (2) the Banana Company massacre, and (3) the strikes and executions.

Before her death, Úrsula shrinks into a fetus shape which resembles "a cherry raisin lost inside of her nightgown." She is found dead on Good Friday morning, but no one is certain of her age, whether she is one hundred and fifteen or one hundred and twenty-two. At her death, the plague of dead birds begins.

Pilar Ternera

The other woman of significance is Pilar Ternera. Among the original founders of Macondo, her parents took her there to separate her from a man who raped her at fourteen "and continued to love her until she was twenty-two." Pilar comes to the Buendía house as a chore girl, but soon begins to read their futures in her cards. She becomes the mistress of the Buendía sons — first of José Arcadio II, then of Aureliano. She bears Arcadio to José Arcadio II, and she is the mother of Aureliano José by the Colonel. When Macondo is infected with the insomnia plague, she adds to the confusion by devising a scheme of reading the past in the same cards that she had previously read the future. We are told that this practice leads to an imaginary reality for Macondians, a reality "which was less practical for them but more comforting." In her predictions, Pilar is always proven right by subsequent events. As she forecasts, Rebeca is never to be happy until her parents are in their graves. In addition, Pilar warns Aureliano Buendía about food poisoning and warns him that his son Aureliano is not to attend the play where he will be assassinated.

Pilar's son Arcadio is raised by the Buendías; he never learns that Pilar Ternera is his mother. Once, he tries to seduce her but she escapes by paying Sofía de la Piedad to become his mistress. Aureliano José has the same attraction to her as his brother, Arcadio, does but he discovers that she is his mother. When this revelation occurs the two become very close, "accomplices in solitude."

Pilar is summed up best in terms of her wasted beauty. In her old age she becomes madam of a local brothel but "never charges for the service" of loaning her room: "She never refused the favor just as she never refused the countless men who sought her out even in the twilight of her maturity, without giving money to lose and only occasionally pleasure." During her lifetime, in addition to her sons, she has five daughters, who are described as having her same hot blood.

During the long time when Amaranta Buendía is knitting her shroud, Pilar Ternera becomes — in the dying woman's eyes — the embodiment of death. Meme, the daughter of Fernanda and Aureliano Segundo, goes to Pilar Ternera for advice on her affair with Mauricio Babilonia, but she fails to recognize that "the centarian witch was her grandmother." In old age, Pilar Ternera is always ultimately linked to the Buendías and their problems. Similarly, Aureliano Segundo goes to her to seek relief for the lump in his throat that is strangling him to death.

Pilar Ternera lives to be one hundred and forty-five years old; she appears finally as a madam comforting the melancholy Aureliano Babilonia. She dies in her rocking chair and, in accordance with her wishes, is buried in the rocker under the center of the brothel dance floor. There, in her tomb, "the sins of the past would rot."

THEMES AND MOTIFS

SOLITUDE

Almost without exception, the Buendía males are marked, as it were, with this tragic sign. And perhaps this theme can best be understood if one studies the individual characters themselves. As the most outstanding member of the second generation, for example, Colonel Aureliano Buendía is a perfect example of "solitude." We learn, for example, that adolescence made him silent and solitary, but in fact he was always a refugee, so to speak, in solitude. As the first human being born in Macondo, he is immediately identified as being reluctant to become anything—yet he is, even then, immensely sympathetic with the plight of his misfortunate society. From the very moment of his being a living possibility, we find him to be a silent and withdrawn fetus, "weeping" in Úrsula's womb, weeping as though he were saddened by the prospect of living (perhaps again). He is clairvoyant and possessed of prophetic powers but his supernatural powers are confused by a congenitally misformed emotional development that we know only as being an "incapacity for human love."

This mournful quality is also reflected in the lives of the twins, Aureliano and José Arcadio IV Segundo. In them, we realize the author's special definition of solitude as being not simply a state of social isolation but a special kind of human relationship and, above all, a need. Aureliano Segundo, for instance, is a genial lover of orgies; he is also extremely reckless. Clearly, his escapades spring from a desire to break the unwavering pattern of repetition in his life. He lives between want and plenty, virtue and hypocrisy, and is always confused about the state of his psychological ennui. In his frustration, he feels a neurotic compulsion to dwell on sadness as a means of feeling human. His brother, José Arcadio IV Segundo, does not have that kind of self-pity and is not wanton in satisfying his appetites. Nevertheless, José Arcadio IV is condemned to live apart from the other Buendías—no matter what he does. Psychologically, José Arcadio IV is always a stranger; nobody knows anything about his life. He is fanatical in his reaction against injustice; at the same time, he enjoys the cruel sport of cockfighting and takes a morbid pleasure in recalling a day when he witnessed human executions when he was only a child. He is a man without an emotional family, imprisoned in sad memories of people's confusing him with his brother—but never, so it appears to him, being able to escape sharing a common fate. Solitude for José Arcadio IV is a reaction to the frustration that he finds in his dual nature and in his confused identity. This frustration is symbolic of the twins' relationship, for, even though they have developed differently and have been shaped by different circumstances, and even though they have lost their physical resemblance, they still meet death at the same time—after a melancholy, solitary period; and, almost as if García Márquez wanted to sharpen the ironic dimension of the twins' relationship, he has each of them buried in the other twin's grave. The twins appear to have been drawn together throughout their lives by an affinity of sadness, emotional impermeability, and by some unnamed, fantastic, inexplicable force.

In a similar way, the relationship between José Arcadio V and his nephew, Aureliano Babilonia, has a sad, Faulknerian cast, filled with the violence and love-hate complexity of two generations of Bonds (a family in Faulkner's *Absalom, Absalom!*). José Arcadio V, arriving home from Rome, senses a rival for Fernanda's estate in the person of the mild, gentle Aureliano. The tension tightens, but after Aureliano saves José Arcadio V's life, they make a kind of truce. There is a kind of mutual tolerance between the two men, but there is no real affection; it is, in fact, a relationship of accommodation, not a fully human relationship, one defined by compassion, but rather one of mechanical action and reaction. As with the twins, we see that here again solitude becomes even a "force of habit" between two people. Clearly, in García Márquez' view, solitude is inevitable; in its redundancy, social habituation impoverishes the emotional strength of even the closest of familial relationships. All the major characters in *One Hundred Years of Solitude* end in that peculiar form of social despair, stagnant under a melancholic illusion that makes them oblivious to the spell of their social and psychological isolation.

FANTASY

In *One Hundred Years of Solitude*, fantasy functions, for the most part, as parody. The official lies of the banana company, as well as Fernanda's delusions of being a queen, are both powerful examples of how even frustrated ambition ultimately leads a person to succumb to a life of fantasy. As critic D. P. Gallagher has observed, fantasy serves here to highlight "absurd but logical exaggerations of real situations . . . [and] the exuberant use of hyperbole in the language of the novel can be seen as a reaction to officialdom." Fantasy, because it both depends upon and disregards factual memory, achieves its special effect through the kind of associations that we make when experiencing a hitherto improbable relationship between symbols of familiar meaning. Here, in the fiction of García Márquez, fantasy becomes symbolic of our time-bound rationalist illusions. José Arcadio I's solution to the insomnia plague, for example, is to simply label everything with inked signs. But that in itself is not enough to ensure that people will remember the thing's function, as well. And after things have been named and the primary functions have been identified, the names of things have to be placed within the context of the things' function; and those instructions have to be related to some other thing's function. Clearly, this leads us back to the story of the world, or, in the case of the novel, the resumption of the story of the Buendías and Macondo. On the other hand, Pilar Ternera's reading of the past in the pattern of her cards becomes as reliable as her fortune telling concerning events in the future; in neither case does she tell enough to make her information credible. Without knowing the specific context of her abstract formulas, people who take her advice sink ever deeper into a fantastic world of illogical relationships. History, in fact, is a record of the loss of a real context; each of us, as we age, loses ever more of the real truth of the past that has changed, and history remains finally as only a skeletal form without our memory. The insomnia plague, José Arcadio I's solution to combat it, and Pilar Ternera's future and history cards — all of these reveal how tightly progress in one direction is ultimately but the extenuation of one direction of history among an infinite number of possible lines of development. We understand also in those instances how illusory is the meaning of anything called eternally real and eternally true. Clearly one form or one formulation of any true statement is true only insofar as it can be abstracted from the real circumstances which would make it contingent and unique. The "fortunes" of Pilar Ternera's prophetic cards, for example, become true but we do not know how; hence, prophecy and the astrological form of predictions are, alike, mere identities or convenient symbols to describe what was not expected but which was, nevertheless, already named. It takes little reflection to realize that whatever happens, in the sense of a future event, will enter the social consciousness — and become news — in the same way. The line between real truth and true fantasy is thus formed by our linear perspective of history — and that is always its limitation: we can never know the whole present — which would be, precisely, the chaotic, random, and exaggerated kind of world that García Márquez describes in this novel. In short, contrary to common sense, we may be rational creatures not by choice but as a necessary adaptation to a world that is always fantastic and beyond our immediate comprehension. To paraphrase the gypsy Melquíades, "the world has a life of its own."

CYCLICAL TIME AND FATE

Aureliano Segundo enters the novel midway – just before he dies – remembering events that are *yet* to be narrated. We come to know his story, then, as a retrospective future that parallels the beginning of the novel's main plot. This chronological reversal of the novel's various plots is a standard flashback technique, but in García Márquez' hands the technique makes the characters always a bit sad, even in the most comic scenes. The Segundo twins, for instance, share cyclical, parallel fates but the reader is always aware that they will fulfill the Macondo legacy of tragic forerunners, doomed to failure and solitude even as they achieve a perpetuation of the Buendía line. In the recurrent disasters of Macondo, the survival of the Buendía line becomes less a hope than a curse; and madness alone permits one to escape the despair of inevitable tragedy. By becoming insane, the patriarch, José Arcadio Buendía I, can thus repair his past mistakes by befriending one of his murder victims who has become a ghost, and throughout his life, by transforming Macondo into a perfect yet solitary community; in short, insanity has its own necessities and logical realities, and in some forms it may be not altogether involuntary. To the extent that one can cultivate an insane view of the world, it is highly probable that insanity is occasionally an adaptation to an intolerable condition or state of mind. In other words, madness may free a person of the social restraints and perceptual values of sane people. Its tragedy, however, resides in a conclusion observed by the Scottish psychologist R. D. Laing: "even a mad world has its own tyrannical set of rules." Therein lies the failure of the mad José Arcadio Buendía I. In the "real" world of Macondo, the prophecies that are penned by Melquíades ultimately become laws, and history, as the ultimate law, is reversible and so must recur. José Arcadio I tries to escape the prophecies of the parchment manuscript, knowing all the while that they have already been fulfilled in another language (life). The reader, of course, knows that the prophecies are the plot of the novel; nonetheless, we must read the novel to know how the plot develops, just as José Arcadio I and, in a larger metaphysical sense, all people must live their lives in the certainty of inevitable death. It is of special significance here to mention that the last adult Buendía realizes, as he is about to complete the translation of the parchment manuscript, that he makes the destruction of Macondo and the Buendías certain by imbuing life, in the act of discovery, into things that were dead already. The novel's ending is partly ambiguous because we are told that everything in the parchment manuscript was unrepeatable but foreseen; and that there is no story until we are actually reading it. To read fiction makes real the symbols of life. That conclusion is both an expression of the author's sense of humor and his philosophy of life, for in Macondo life continues from one generation to the next by a kind of translation of the same message, the same events, and the same characters. The Colonel embarks on a life of political rebellion out of the same vague fear of destiny that obsessed his father. And the same sense of frantic desperation, the sense that things have always been out of control, emerges in the patriarch's aging daughter Amaranta. After Death requests that she begin to make her shroud by a certain day, she stalls in the hope that by prolonging her task she can somehow delay the day when she will die. On the deadline date, however, she embraces her fate as if, in doing so, she freely chooses what will happen to her regardless of its inevitability. The question is moot whether or not we are free to choose to accept an inevitable fate. The characters in *One Hundred Years of Solitude* only seem mad when they think they can change their destiny; in a retrospective view, however, many historical personages appear the same way, a view perhaps best summed up in the saying "Nothing really changes."

THE SENSE OF ILLEGITIMACY

Another obvious theme of García Márquez is the sense of il-legitimacy. In this novel, the logic of incest is always official bastard-ization. This is expressed in the ancient Buendía fear that incest will eventually produce a child with a pig's tail. García Márquez makes that fear a kind of self-fulfilling prophecy; incest leads to illegitimacy, inter-family rivalry, and a sense of inferiority about their paternity. The women, like Fernanda, create a glorious illusion of their past, and they never dwell on the negative aspects of it. On the other hand, the sense of inferiority in the bastard Buendía males tarnishes any achievement or virtue that they may come to have. In their obses-sion, we see the long-standing sense of inferiority that Latin America has been made to feel in her relation to the Anglo-American North. Necessary but despised, this South American twin continent of North

America has found her brilliant, enigmatic past, present, and future muted in the soiled obscurity of her origins.

MACHISMO VS HEROISM

Machismo (the need to express one's masculinity through brute force, sexual profligacy, proliferation of male heirs, and subjugation of others – especially women) is a quintessential trait of the Buendías. Machismo is both responsible for their gallantry and for their courage, as well as being responsible for their suicidal persistence in the face of certain failure. Note, in particular, the posturing and the false pride of the Colonel. All the Buendía males seem compelled in one way or another to prove themselves through exaggerated acts of sexual, bodily, and militaristic appetite – as if mere physical capacity was itself a measure of heroism. Like the Colonel (in García Márquez' short novel *No One Writes to The Colonel*), the Buendía males seem motivated to try quixotic tests of adversity – out of fear. They engage in cruel cockfights and reckless gambling because they have long ago become complacent to foreign and domestic forms of political exploitation, as well as almost constant unemployment. Most of the time they rebel against the injustice of their lives not out of any clear moral indignation but, rather, out of idleness. And they tolerate cruelty, not only to men and the abused Buendía women, but to the fighting cocks as well; they have learned to accept the political cruelty imposed on themselves. The Colonel's reaction to the Conservative regime leads only to a situation wherein Macondo and her people have been battered to the point of collapse. His heroism and grand compassion, in fact, make no difference to the lives that he intends to uplift. Ultimately, even his battles and his existence – his historical moment – have no meaning. The Buendías are seldom truly heroic; more often than not they are reckless, and thus they rebel, as did Arcadio José IV Segundo, after the fact of the massacre, or, as with the patriarch himself, after falling victim to insult.

PROPHECY

We learn that adolescence made Aureliano (the last adult Buendía) silent and "definitely solitary." His brooding demeanor strikes both an echo and a foreboding in our minds: we sense in his tension that something will soon occur. He is always quiet and subdued. But he apprehends future events intuitively, and his gift of prophecy becomes the motive for all his later misadventures. His affair with Amaranta Úrsula, for example, fulfills the prophetic curse of Buendía incest. It is through Aureliano that we realize how moral history and destiny impinge. In completing the decipherment of the ancient Sanskrit manuscript of Melquíades, he realizes the conclusion of the history of the Buendías in the act of reading. Here, action is time; and art is, in Faulkner's sense of the word, potential time – that is, it only becomes actual through our experiencing it. Through his work, the artist creates the possibility of a simultaneous dimension of time; his dead symbols come to life whenever we feel recognizable meaning in them. And some meaning for us is always present in García Márquez' narrative, no matter who reads or creates it. In this sense, everyone has a foreordained future.

ESSAY TOPICS

A. Short Topics

1. Explain possible answers for the Buendías' limited capacity for love.

2. Contrast the concepts of solitude and solidarity through one generation of the Buendía family.

3. Comment on the stability of the Buendía women, when compared with the Buendía males.

4. What part does fantasy play within the novel?

B. Long Topics

1. Explain the Buendías' inordinate fear of punishment because of incest.

2. Discuss the role of illegitimacy within the Buendía family and García Márquez' attitude towards South America.

3. How successfully is solitude used as a metaphor for the Buendías' "curse," and how successfully can it be applied to South
America's historically lesser role in the politics of the Western
world?

4. Why is this novel more successful as a "myth" than it would
have been if it had been told in chronological order with actual dates and names and places?

SELECTED BIBLIOGRAPHY

Books by Gabriel García Márquez (in English translation)

The Autumn of the Patriarch. trans. Gregory Rabassa. Harper & Row,
1978.

The Incredible and Sad Tale of Innocent Erendira and Other Stories. trans.
Gregory Rabassa. Harper & Row, 1978.

The Evil Hour. trans. Gregory Rabassa. Harper & Row, 1979.

Leaf Storm and Other Stories. trans. Gregory Rabassa. Harper & Row,
1979.

No One Writes to the Colonel and Other Stories. trans. Gregory Rabassa.
Harper & Row, 1968.

One Hundred Years of Solitude. trans. Gregory Rabassa. Harper & Row,
1970.

Chronicle of a Death Foretold. trans. Gregory Rabassa. Alfred A. Knopf,
1983.

Critical Books and Articles

CIPLIJAUSKAITE, BIRUTE. "Foreshadowing as Technique and Theme in
One Hundred Years of Solitude." *Books Abroad* 47, 3 (1973):
466-70.

CHRIST, RONALD. Review of *Leaf Storm and Other Stories, Commonweal,* 9/22/72: 504.

DAUSTER, FRANK. "The Short Stories of García Márquez." *Books Abroad,* 47, 3 (1973): 466-70.

DUFF, MARTHA. "Back to Macondo," review of *Leaf Storm and Other Stories, Time,* 3/13/72.

FOSTER, DAVID WILLIAM. "Gabriel García Márquez and Solitude." *Americas* 21 (1969): 36-41.

GALLAGHER, D. P. *Modern Latin American Literature.* Oxford University Press. 1973.

GUIBERT, RITA. "Gabriel García Márquez." In *Seven Voices.* Alfred A. Knopf, 1973, pp. 305-37.

HARSS, LUIS and BARBARA DOHMANN. "Gabriel García Márquez, or the Lost Chord." In *Into the Mainstream.* Harper & Row, 1967, pp. 310-41.

HOWES, VICTOR. "South American Gothic: 'Ivy Invades the Houses.' " *Christian Science Monitor.* 2/24/72.

KAZIN, ALFRED. "Leaf Storm and Other Stories." *New York Times Book Review.* 2/20/72. pp. 11-14.

KENNEDY, WILLIAM. "The Yellow Trolley Car in Barcelona and Other Visions." *Atlantic Monthly* 231, 1 (1973): 50-59.

KIELY, ROBERT. "One Hundred Years of Solitude." *New York Times Book Review,* 3/8/70. p. 5.

LEONARD, JOHN. "Myth is Alive in Latin America." *New York Times.* 3/3/70. p. 43.

LOCKE, RICHARD. "Márquez' Magical Mysteries," *New York Times.* 3/17/72.

70

MEAD, ROBERT G. "For Sustenance: Hope." *Saturday Review*. 12/21/68.

MYERS, OLIVER T. "No One Writes to the Colonel." *The Nation*. 12/2/68.

OBERHELMAN, HARLEY D. "García Márquez and the American South." *Chasqui*, V, 1 (1975): 29-38.

PEEL, ROGER M. "The Short Stories of Gabriel García Márquez." *Studies in Short Fiction*, 8 (1971): 159-68.

PRESCOTT, PETER S. "Miracles and Mysteries." *Newsweek*. 2/28/72.

RABASSA, GREGORY. "Beyond Magical Realism: Thoughts on the Art of Gabriel García Márquez." *Books Abroad*. 47, 3 (1973): 442-50.

RICHARDSON, JACK. "Master Builder: *One Hundred Years of Solitude* by Gabriel García Márquez." *New York Review of Books*, 3/26/70, pp. 3-4.

ROLFE, DORIS. "The Novels of Gabriel García Márquez." *Graduate Studies on Latin America*. University of Kansas, 1973, pp. 63-75.

SHORRIS, EARL. "Gabriel García Márquez: The Alchemy of History." *Harper's Magazine*, 244. 2/72. pp. 98-102.

TOBIN, PATRICIA. "García Márquez and the Subversion of the Line." *Latin American Literary Review*, II, 4 (1974): 39-48.

A compilation of most of the English language reviews of Gabriel García Márquez' works can be found in *70 Review*, ed. Ronald Christ, Center for Inter-American Relations, Inc., 1970. See also: *Gabriel García Márquez* by George R. McMurray (Frederick Ungar Publishing Co., 1977) for a general overview of the complete stories.